ADHD

How to go from powerless professional to powerhouse leader

GWENDOLYN JANSSEN

B₂B

To Little Bear, Fluffernutter, Doc, and Little Madre.
All that I am is because of you.

First published in 2023 by Gwendolyn Janssen

© Gwendolyn Janssen 2023

The moral rights of the author have been asserted

ISBN: 978-1-922764-96-6

Library of Congress Control Number: 2023908349

Book production and text design by Publish Central
Cover design by Pipeline Design

Disclaimer

Contents

Acknowledgements

It is a privilege to acknowledge the following people who influenced, inspired, and supported the creation of this book:

Veronica Striffler—My number one fan and the embodiment of unconditional love. Thank you for always being by my side, bringing meaning and purpose to this life, and for never giving up on me, even when I want to give up on myself.

Bonnie Solitaire—The truest definition of a leader I have ever known and one of my best friends. I did not know what it was to lead until I was led by you. Thank you for always believing in me and never letting me forget that I am better than my worst days.

Trish Horlacher—My dear friend. We have been kindred spirits from day one, and I will never be able to repay you for showing me what it means to be loved for everything that I am and nothing less. Your guidance, wisdom, and friendship mean everything. Thank you for never giving up on me.

Vina Delgado, Crystal Martinez, and Heather Garcia—As tumultuous as it was when we were a team, there is no one I would rather have weathered the storm with than the three of you. You have taught me to lead with grace, authenticity, passion, and grit. I hope I never let you forget that the only reason I did not drown in those waters is because of the unwavering love and support you all showed me. I did not do a thing to deserve any of you, but I am so incredibly lucky to have women like you to love me when I am thoroughly unlovable. Thank you for always being a shining reminder that you can do anything with the right people by your side.

Kath Walters—Writing a book is such an intimate process, and I cannot imagine having trusted it with anyone but you, Kath. Your patience, support, empathy, and guidance mean more than I can ever express. Thank you for helping me achieve this incredible goal. Here's to many more books to come.

Andrew Bordt—You were among the first to reach out in a show of support and solidarity after I announced my diagnosis. Thank you for welcoming me to the neurodiverse community and sharing your wisdom with me.

Brooke Schnittman—Thank you for giving up so many Monday morning commutes to share your wisdom and expertise. You are a mentor, a leader, a trailblazer, and an amazing human.

Becca King—Thank you for being such a kind and wonderful person who gives up your time and shares your knowledge. The work you do hits home for me; you are truly a gift to the ADHD community.

George Eastwood—Third time's the charm. Thank you for giving up your time and sharing your expertise in serving the neuro-diverse community. Your passion for your work shines in everything you do.

Introduction

Reflecting on the course of your professional career and your time as a leader, how many of the following describe your journey thus far?

- A myriad of misunderstandings.
- Constant miscommunications, despite your best efforts.
- Frustrations when nothing seems to click. You don't know why because it is not for lack of trying.
- Feeling "unfit".
- Always being told you are "not enough" of this or "too much" of that.
- Feeling passionate but lost.
- Being undervalued.
- Wondering why your weaknesses seem to find their way to the spotlight, but your strengths don't get the attention they deserve.
- Struggling to stay engaged over long periods or lots of job changes.

- Feeling like you missed the boat or missed your calling.
- Endless classes, books, training, education, and workshops aimed at leadership development that never really hit the mark for you.

Sound familiar? My dear friend, this book is for you. This list encompasses countless situations across my lifespan and over 15 years as a healthcare professional. I have been a bedside nurse to a multi-unit nursing director, a preceptor to an adjunct professor, an avid reader and now a writer. All this time never quite fitting in and never understanding why. It was not until age 33, when I was diagnosed with ADHD, that I gained the clarity I had searched for my entire life. Fast forward to today, where you hold this book in your hands because you know what this struggle feels like and you know you deserve better. I know you do too, and I will show you how to get it.

When I was almost finished writing this book, I had an ugly crying meltdown with my book coach, Kath Walters, in our one-on-one session. Earlier that day, in my last work meeting before signing off for Thanksgiving, I was asked, "You keep saying you want to be a leader, but you do X, Y, Z. Do you really think that is how a leader should behave?"

I have been questioned like this for as long as I can remember. Yet, no matter how often I hear it, I am cut to the core each time. This type of question reminds me that in many places, ADHD is treated as a dysfunction—something to be eradicated, not celebrated. For the rest of that night and most of the next day, I had no confidence in my ability to lead, perform as a professional, and write this book. As I cried to Kath over Zoom, I told her I felt like a fraud. What business did I have writing a book about leadership when, even now, I was seen as unfit?

The moment that question was asked, I was caught off guard. I resorted to masking and agreeing with the judgment placed on me. All I could say was, "I can see how that would not be appropriate leadership behavior." But on reflection, after a good night's sleep and a lot of self-care, I was reaffirmed in my *real* belief. Leaders *must* be honest. They *must* be authentic. They *must not* be afraid to talk about the things that aren't going right as long as they are willing to commit to being part of the solution. Leadership means addressing challenges head-on without sugarcoating or falsehoods. We can never hope to achieve the exceptional if we do not acknowledge when we're missing the mark. So yes, I think leaders should behave the way I do.

This situation mirrors so many I have had in my leadership journey—never quite right, but not sure why. My ADHD diagnosis helped many missing pieces fall into place when I reflected on my professional and leadership struggles. That doesn't mean that I never have bad days when my perspective is misunderstood, but it does mean that I recover faster from those days now. I do not allow the neurotypical view of the world to make me ashamed of who I am. My hope is that this book gives you the clarity, understanding, acceptance, support, and guidance you deserve. I hope you find a home within these pages. You have been spinning your wheels for too long and investing time, energy, and money into tools not built for your brain. In understanding how ADHD can make you a powerhouse leader, you unlock potential where there was struggle; development where there was despair.

I have been in healthcare my entire career. From a young age, I was lucky to know I wanted to be a nurse, and I pursued that goal with an unwavering passion. A few years into that career, I was offered the opportunity to move into leadership, and it was there that I found my calling. Despite my passion and dedication to being a good leader, I had to fight tooth and nail in almost every position I held. Working hard to be what others always told me leaders "should" be. But no matter what methods, tactics, and tools I put into place, I still never felt I fit the leadership mold. My style and potential have been questioned at almost every stage of my career.

I know the value ADHD leaders bring to the table. My mission is to make it easier for you to achieve your leadership goals. I will give you tools and tips tailored to the ADHD brain. Despite what you have been told, you *are* enough. You have everything you need to be an exceptional leader/entrepreneur already inside you. Having ADHD comes with challenges when navigating a world that wasn't built for us. Still, there are so many strengths and unique benefits to your brain wiring that will benefit you as a leader. Your brain moves fast, and I will show you how to use that to help you move forward.

Get ready to cover a veritable smorgasbord of tips, tactics, and tales of success and struggle that will lead (no pun intended . . . Ok, maybe pun intended a little) to you performing optimally as the head of a team, department, service line, or company. The sky's the limit when you unlock your potential; together we will help you fly.

1

ADHD and Me

Introduction

You may have lived the majority of your life never once considering that you might have Attention-Deficit/Hyperactivity Disorder (ADHD). Like me and so many others, you think you know what ADHD looks like, and it doesn't look like you, right? Well, if the introduction resonated with you, you might have a professional history littered with moments where you knew, "I'm not like other leaders, but I am not sure why." You almost always feel like you have to work ten times harder than anyone else just to get half as far. Your differences may have prevented you from realizing your career ambitions. Sound familiar? Welcome to the world of living and leading with ADHD.

Disclaimer (so our friends in legal don't come after me with torches and pitchforks): While I am a nurse, I have never specialized in neurology or behavioral health and do not claim any level of *clinical* expertise in these areas. What I am is a leader with ADHD—undiagnosed until age 33—writing about my experience after doing lots and lots (and lots) of research. With the help of this book, I want you to turn your leadership ambitions into reality with far fewer trials and tribulations than I've experienced.

I have found that most people do not comprehensively understand what ADHD is, so let's start there. The well-known American research and medical organization the Mayo Clinic (2019) defines ADHD as "a chronic condition . . . [that] includes a combination of persistent problems, such as difficulty sustaining attention, hyperactivity and impulsive behavior." You may not recognize yourself in that definition or experience an "Aha!" moment but stay with me. In Chapter Two, I will go into much greater detail on the symptoms and presentations of ADHD based on research and my personal experience. What you learn there might just be your "Aha!" moment. In a literature review published in 2014 by Dr. Ylva Ginsberg et al. titled "Underdiagnosis of Attention-Deficit/Hyperactivity Disorder in Adult Patients: A Review of the Literature", some researchers estimate that over 80 percent of adults with ADHD remain undiagnosed and/or untreated. It is not improbable to believe that you could fall into that large majority.

You may have put a lot of time and energy into fighting your ADHD presentations, although you may not realize it. You combat your natural tendencies, develop compensatory mechanisms for your struggles, and are left frustrated because no matter how many books you read, programs you complete, or degrees you achieve, it never seems enough. But what if the answer was right there all along?

What if you were given the roadmap to your leadership ambitions and career goals? You have that map in hand. Within these pages is the key to leading with ADHD.

To start, you need to gain the comprehensive understanding of ADHD you may have lacked. To be frank, you cannot optimize what you do not understand. Recognizing that you have ADHD allows you to put a name and frame to your experiences. It gives you the clarity and direction you have been lacking. Your energy and time are precious commodities. You do not need to waste them on a hamster wheel of misinformation, misunderstanding, and misplaced efforts.

As our 80 percent statistic highlights, just because no one has ever suspected that you have ADHD (including you) does not mean you don't have it. Adult diagnosis of ADHD has seen a substantial increase as doctors learn more about the condition. Prevalence reports vary, but the 2019 study by Dr. Winston Chung et al. published in the *Journal of the American Medical Association* (also known as *JAMA*, the most widely circulated medical journal in the world) shows that from 2007 to 2016, the prevalence of diagnosed adult ADHD rose by over 123 percent. Chapter Four is dedicated to discussing diagnosis, but it is important to note that it is not just possible but quite common to reach adulthood without a diagnosis. Currently, there are three presentations of ADHD recognized by the medical community: hyperactive/impulsive; predominantly inattentive; and combined. These will be covered in more detail in Chapter Two. A quick note, as it may shed light on why so many patients reach adulthood without being diagnosed.

Inattentive and combined type ADHD tend to have fewer physical hyperactivity symptoms than hyperactive/impulsive type. Meaning others may perceive individuals with inattentive or combined type as less "disruptive" than those with hyperactive type. It is not a huge leap to surmise that the less people were "bothered" by you as a child, the higher the likelihood that your symptoms will be unrecognized and undiagnosed as ADHD.

So far, I've told you a little about me, but now we will dig deeper. I want to share my story of a lifetime of disconnection, misunderstandings, and labeling, and the impact of perception and judgment. Let me know if you can relate.

Leaders don't cry

Like me, you may have been told you are not leadership material, and maybe you even started to believe it. Emotional dysregulation (frequent and sometimes unexplained changes in your mood and an inability to control your emotional responses) has caused others to view you as unprofessional, weak, sensitive, immature, or unstable. Managing your time and priorities takes an excessive amount of brain power, leaving you drained and still missing deadlines. You forget details and dates despite knowing how important they are. You sometimes feel overwhelmed by even the smallest task, but do your best work when you have procrastinated to the last minute because now it's crunch time. Is any of this ringing a bell? ADHD is a type of neurodiversity that causes you to experience the world and express your emotions differently than your neurotypical peers. When you and those around you do not understand how to optimize those differences, it can lead everyone to assume that you just don't have what it takes.

You have goals, dreams, and ambitions that will remain unfulfilled if you do not become intimately acquainted with how your brain operates and how that operation translates into your interactions with the world. You may suffer from low self-esteem, self-doubt, and overall disengagement if these goals and dreams continue to be unrealized. Want to stop leaving so much untapped talent and potential on the table? Maybe it's time to consider that you may have ADHD.

I remember the first time I was pointedly told that I wasn't a leader. I was 18, a senior in high school, getting ready to head off to my top-choice undergraduate program in nursing. Our school district had a unique program for a small, select group of students spanning grades 9 to 12. You had to apply to get in and were permitted to join no later than your freshman or sophomore year. The classes were specific in their intent—to replicate college-level course content and design. Once accepted to this program, you spent all 4 years with that same group of students. You took almost every single class together, every annual field trip together, and spent most of your time at school surrounded by these people. Needless to say, you got to know everyone well. As we were nearing graduation, we were asked to evaluate one another. A smaller version of a 360-degree evaluation in which you provide anonymous feedback to your peers. The intent was to help us better understand ourselves before entering the big, wide world.

When I opened the summary of the feedback that had been given about me, there were all of the parts of myself that I hated right there in black and white.

"She is distracting in class because of her emotional outbursts."

"Hard to focus because when Gwen is upset, everyone knows about it."

"Always all over the place and challenging to get along with because she can't control her moods."

My emotional reaction to this feedback was a deep shame. I blamed myself for all these flaws I didn't feel I could control—just another demonstration of how my peers didn't understand me and a reminder that I didn't understand myself. I started to cry. The program director, one of our science teachers, stood up at the front of the room and addressed the group.

"How you receive these evaluations and what you do with this information says a lot about you. Leaders don't cry when reading feedback they don't like."

I was the only one crying, and her words hit me like a freight train. Why couldn't I be stable and normal like everyone else? Why didn't anyone see that I didn't *want* to be this way and that I was desperate for help? What hope did I ever have of becoming a leader if, even at 18, I was told I didn't make the cut?

Are you one of those professionals thinking, "Gwen, leaders *don't* cry. To be effective, they must be level-headed and in control of their emotions at all times."? I can understand the argument for that sentiment. However, I firmly believe there is a place for managed emotional displays in the workplace. In recent years there has been a shift, redefining what it means to be a leader. Now, they must have higher emotional intelligence than ever. Your ability to demonstrate emotion shows humanity and humility while building trust with those working for you and alongside you. Of course, not everyone is comfortable crying in front of others, but we have to stop looking at it as career suicide if a leader does.

If you're stubborn, you might counterargue that these displays should be saved for when you are at home or in a therapist's office. Have you considered that being in tune with our emotions and learning how to display them in effective ways takes a lot of introspection and effort? These are qualities that belong at work without question. As you improve your self-awareness through emotional intelligence, you demonstrate your dedication to growth and development, both critical pursuits for any leader.

What if this doesn't sound like you? Does that eliminate you from the running? Nope. Nice try, though. I have a dear friend, Dr. Heather Garcia, a healthcare leader and one of the most even-keeled individuals I know. She also happens to have ADHD. She's a "do-no-harm-but-take-no-shit" type of person. I have never heard her raise her voice, I can't recall a time I saw her cry, and I am always amazed by her ability to maintain calm in even the most stressful environments. Some people, even with ADHD, can interact with the world in a more reserved manner at baseline. Heather is the perfect example of how differently ADHD can present from person to person. She and I are very different leaders, but our brain wiring helps make us each a powerhouse in our own right.

For some ADHDers, the ability to appear outwardly unemotional (or at least less emotional) can be the result of years (sometimes decades) of what is known as masking—hiding your ADHD symptoms from others. You aim to behave and communicate in ways that align with neurotypical and societal norms. You have always been told that you are just "too much", so you try to be less.

I applaud you if calm, cool, and collected is your natural state. However, if it results from masking, I encourage you to dig deeper into your emotions and work toward unmasking in a safe space. We will talk more about this later. For now, it is important to know that working toward showing up authentically can reduce the risk of burnout and identity crisis often associated with masking. It is important to allow yourself the space to work through uncomfortable feelings and learn how to process and express them in healthy and cathartic ways. You can accomplish this with the help of a therapist, a clinical psychologist or another trained mental health professional. You will also find help right here. The last three chapters of this book serve as a "how-to" starter guide for ADHD leaders, and Chapter Nine is dedicated to helping you manage emotions with ADHD.

Let's reflect. When was the last time you were told or were made to feel like you could not or should not be a leader? If you played sports, were you ever chosen as the team captain? Are you recommended or nominated by others to serve as project lead at work? Have you ever been offered official leadership opportunities?

You may have conditioned yourself to believe that others are right when they say you are not leadership material. They tell you how you present yourself is a far cry from what the ideal leader looks like. When people tell you often enough what you are and are not, you start to believe them. Let me be the first to call bullshit on that. Those people that love to hold you down instead of helping you up, I believe we call them mean girls.

Is that a knife in your back?

Ah, the mean girls club. You know the feeling. You're being judged and evaluated at every turn, but no one says so to your face. Excluded from conversations, it is not hard to recognize when colleagues, bosses, or direct reports are talking behind your back. Significant judgment without any attempt at empathy or under-standing. Nice, right? I love the feeling of knives in my back. Okay, I admit that was macabre and melodramatic, but in reality, human beings love to demonize what they don't understand. They create distance and separation to avoid being lumped in with the "unde-sirables". Humans have done it since the dawn of time.

Consider this Stephen Covey quote shared by one of my favorite professors, Dr. Amer Kaissi (who also happens to be an exceptional executive coach, public speaker, and author): "We judge ourselves by our intentions and others by their actions." Ooph. Reality check coming in hot. It sucks, but it is true. We rush to judge only by what we see and often presume or assume the worst in others. It's more fun than giving them the benefit of the doubt! Ok, enough of my tongue-in-cheek remarks. Let's get real. Like it or not, perceptions can make or break your leadership potential. Negative perceptions are often the result of misunderstandings. So how do we fix that? For starters, *you* have to understand yourself. When you understand yourself, you are well prepared to help others understand you.

Let's translate that into real life. At 29 years old, I accepted my first director position. It was one of the most challenging positions I have ever held. Why? Largely, because of a few colleagues and direct reports who found it easier to talk about me instead of to me. Add to the mix a boss who saw me as a problem to be dealt with instead of a person to be developed. To be fair, I had a lot of growing to do. I admit I made many mistakes in that role and was far from perfect, but I held a deep passion for taking great care of our people and patients. Despite my effort, the hours I worked, and the unwavering dedication I showed, it was never enough. I laughed too loud, talked too much, drank water the wrong way (yep, that was a genuine complaint brought against me), never dressed right, and was always too much this and not enough that.

A colleague once reported me to my boss because she felt I had not conducted myself professionally in an interview with a director candidate for one of our departments. I recall on the day of the interview, I was tired but didn't feel angry, upset or frustrated. In the group interview, I thought I asked appropriate questions and engaged with the candidate meaningfully. My colleague's perspective was unbelievably different. I was called to my VP's office, where my colleague sat waiting. I was told that my behavior was embarrassing to the entire team and so inappropriate that my colleague almost walked out of the interview because she couldn't tolerate my conduct. My VP took it a step further and said I was jeopardizing the hospital's success because I was scaring away qualified candidates (the VP was not present during interview but was going off my colleague's report).

No one said a word to me during or after the interview, or even later that day. In following up with the other directors who were present, none of them felt I had been inappropriate or rude. Still, my colleague's account was damning enough to light a match under my (professional) funeral pyre. It's important to note, the candidate did end up taking the job and had a much longer tenure with that team than I did. When I apologized to her after she was hired, she said that she had no negative feelings about my treatment of her during the interview and at no point did our interaction make her question her decision to join the team.

Soon after, I was again called into my VP's office. I can't even remember the specifics of the concern on that particular day. These visits were increasing in frequency, leaving me beaten down and burned out. I felt like I could not get out from under the microscope, and nothing I did was right. Finally, as my boss reprimanded me for whatever the latest issue happened to be, I reached a breaking point. I asked her, "Is it time we re-evaluate my fit for this role?" Without missing a beat, she looked me dead in the eye and said, "I can promise you it is already being re-evaluated." Another kick to the gut. Another shot against me and my leadership abilities. Another judgment passed without me even understanding why I was on trial.

Are you rolling your eyes at me right now? "Gwen, get off your high horse. Everyone judges everyone. This is not unique to those with ADHD." While that is true, the general lack of understanding of the presentations and symptoms of ADHD can make navigating the workforce and the politics that go along with it even more challenging.

Think back. Have you ever experienced a sense that others were talking about you at work? You might have been given forceful feedback on your performance or conduct as if everyone knew except you. Maybe everyone stops talking when you walk into the room. You feel like you're being left out of conversations or at least encouraged not to participate. You sense that people are pulling away, and you're not sure why.

If you struggle to understand why people may be talking about you instead of with you, check your thoughts with someone you trust. It can be uncomfortable, and seeking feedback can trigger negative emotions or a phenomenon called rejection sensitivity dysphoria (RSD), which we will talk about in Chapter Three. Still, these conversations can be crucial in gaining deeper insight into your colleagues' perceptions.

To build (or rebuild) a positive reputation in the workplace, you need allies. People that see your strengths and can support you when you struggle. Without allies, you have a higher chance of being ostracized by your peers and left out of consideration for promotions. As a result, you may not be offered the same opportunities, or worse, you may be asked to resign or be fired. These can be devastating blows to the ego and self-esteem. Your growth can be hindered, and your potential is squandered as you get back on your feet.

To be clear, ADHD presents differently in everyone, even within the same type. Not every ADHDer has experienced challenges like this. If you are one of the lucky ones in a supportive workplace with colleagues who advocate for you and lift you up, that is wonderful! Hold on to that. My point is that regardless of how we present, we ALL deserve a supportive workplace where we are empowered to embrace our strengths and not forced to mask to get by. The right environment for you is out there. If you haven't found it yet, I encourage you to keep looking because you deserve the opportunity to flourish.

Passed over and pushed out

When you're struggling to stay afloat at work because you're fighting negative perceptions and lack of understanding, your name is probably not on the "promote" list. Being passed over for a promotion or new opportunity you had your heart set on never feels good. It can be devastating when you feel like you've worked as hard as possible to be ready to move up and are still skipped over.

Are you in an endless cycle of chasing the next big thing? Once you accomplish something at work, you're already thinking about what's next. There's a reason for that. When you have ADHD, your brain responds well to novelty—the new and exciting, the challenge, the change of pace. These are sources of dopamine that we are always searching for because our brains have lower baseline levels than our neurotypical counterparts. Novelty and challenge can keep us engaged and energized about our work, resulting in peak performance. So what happens when opportunity never seems to knock for you? You just need to work harder, right? The endless and elusive pursuit of perfectionism.

"If I am the first to show up and the last to leave, they'll notice my commitment."

"If I pore over this presentation again and again, spending hours editing it, they'll see my dedication."

"If I bake homemade goodies for the entire team, they'll see how compassionate I am and want to be my friend."

As unfortunate as it is, none of these steps you're taking bring you closer to the finish line, despite feeling like you've run an ultra-marathon already. The more you do, the less it seems to work. If you continue to be neglected or rejected, the dopamine dwindles. You may become disengaged or lose the passion for leadership that you once had. For obvious reasons, this causes your performance to dip, further diminishing the chances for advancement. Do you feel a bit like Sisyphus? Hades punished this king of Ephyra from Greek mythology for cheating death. Sisyphus was forced to push a boulder to the top of a mountain for eternity, only to have it roll back down every time he reached the summit (sounds pretty awful). It also sounds like many ADHDers I know. They are on the fast track to burnout because their primary focus is trying to prove themselves to people that don't (and won't) understand them. I have been guilty of this myself.

In my first role as a director, some of the people I worked with made me want to walk away from healthcare leadership forever.

Burnout doesn't seem to do justice to what I was feeling. I was so broken when it was all over. "But it couldn't have always been that way. How did it start?" In the beginning, I was bright-eyed and full of hope as a nurse manager. Things weren't bad then. Within six months, I was asked to be the interim director when the previous director was asked to leave. I was interim for a short time before interviewing for and accepting the permanent director position. I was told I was being groomed to become the next VP of the Women's Service Line of the hospital. That was great, but also short-lived. Instead, I was asked to resign from the director role at the end of a year and a half. To go from feeling like they all believed in me and could see a bright future ahead, to being tossed out 18 months later was an ending I didn't see coming until it was too late.

I spent so much time, energy, money, and brain power in that role (and every role since) trying to figure out how to make myself the "right" choice for advancement. All of this was before my ADHD diagnosis so it made little difference. The resources I relied on weren't getting to the root of the struggle: ADHD.

You may think, "If you were passed over, or pushed out, maybe you weren't right for the role or that employer." That's true. Most people can't be a good fit *everywhere*, but this is a matter of not feeling like a good fit *anywhere*. ADHDers often challenge the status quo and like to shake things up in the name of innovation. In the wrong environment, this can be a death sentence. In the right environment, it is evidence of the many valuable skills and traits you bring to the table. As an ADHD leader, creativity, drive, compassion, ingenuity, and empathy (to name a few) can all make you exceptional. With the right support system and environment, these traits come together in beautiful harmony to help you thrive.

Think back to a time that you were passed over or not even considered for a role or an opportunity that you wanted. What qualifications did you have that would've made you a great fit? Was there an explanation given for why you were not chosen? What internal narrative developed as a result? Did you tell yourself you didn't deserve the role and treat the situation as proof that you are not leadership material? These reflections can help you differentiate between the facts and the negative narrative you may be telling yourself about your potential as a result of the way you were treated.

If you are in an environment or team that don't support your growth or leadership ambitions, despite your effort to hone your strengths and balance your areas of opportunity, take some time to process how that feels. We will touch on this more later, but for now, ask yourself, "Am I struggling to move forward because I don't have what it takes or because something or someone is holding me back?"

📋 IN SUMMARY

ADHD can feel like you never quite fit in and you don't know how to change that. Discovering how your brain wiring impacts how you show up in the world is the first step to getting back in the race instead of being stuck on the sidelines. People have told you your whole life that you can't, don't or shouldn't. They didn't understand you, and you didn't either, until now. People will talk about you. Humans are quick to judge and slow to understand. The better you know yourself, the better you can help others understand you to promote a positive perception of yourself as a leader.

I want you to stop thinking there's something wrong with you and that you are unfit or unworthy. Start evaluating your experiences. How much can you relate to the stories I've shared? Was it like looking in a mirror? There is so much stigma around mental health and neurodiversity. Still, there are so many advantageous aspects to the brain wiring that we know as ADHD. It is nothing to be afraid or ashamed of.

I hope your mental wheels are turning because we're just getting started. In the next chapter, we're going to explore the types of ADHD and their presentations, and highlight some traits that can impact your leadership performance. I'll give you insight into some of your "different and don't know whys".

2

Bullet-Train Brain

Introduction

Raise your hand if you feel victimized by the amount of money you have invested into self-improvement with what seems like small returns. You are in good company. In an attempt to become the leader I thought I was supposed to be, I spent an exorbitant amount of time and money on leadership books, development courses, and personal improvement projects. I invested four years and almost US$100K earning two master's degrees—both focused on healthcare leadership and management. While some of these things did help me to grow, nothing provided any significant breakthroughs. I never had the "Aha!" moment I was looking for. Instead, it all left me feeling like I was working hard and gaining no ground.

The general public (and many healthcare providers) are not well versed in the significant nuances and presenting symptoms of ADHD. However, to be an effective leader with ADHD, you cannot afford *not* to be an expert in your brain wiring. In this chapter, I will teach you a lot of what we know about the science of ADHD, talk about the three presentation types in more detail, and discuss the symptoms within each presentation.

Why should you care about all of this? After receiving my diagnosis, I wanted to know more about the pathophysiology of ADHD. I found it helpful to uncover what the researchers and experts understood about my condition. By reviewing the evidence, I received validation that the presentations I struggled with had both an explanation and a firm basis in reality. I want you to feel that validation and certainty too. ADHD is a real condition with a proven scientific foundation. You are not making excuses and do not need to just "try harder".

Research nerd

Despite the work that has been done, there are still some unknowns in the etiology of ADHD. The diagnostic criteria have changed many times, as has the terminology used to define it. So what do we know? For starters, we know the way you experience life and show up in the world reflects a diversity in your brain chemistry, structure, and wiring. In his 2022 article, "ADHD Neuroscience 101" in *ADDitude* magazine, Dr. Larry Silver points out, "We don't know which brain region is the source of ADHD symptoms. Nor can we tell whether the problem lies with a deficiency of norepinephrine itself or of its chemical constituents, dopa and dopamine."

The bottom line is that we still have a lot to learn, but we have discovered some important facts about ADHD brains. These are a few key highlights from the evidence:

- Most researchers agree that a genetic and hereditary link exists between who is born ADHD and who is not (Sherman 2022).
- With ADHD, there is a lower baseline level of the neurotransmitter dopamine (Seay and Ratey 2022)
  - There is also a deficiency of the neurotransmitter norepinephrine (synthesized in the brain from dopamine) (Silver 2022).
- Dopamine receptors in ADHD brains are significantly decreased (Szeto 2019).
- With ADHD, there are altered functional connectivity and activity profiles within different regions of the brain (Silver 2022):
  - *The frontal cortex* orchestrates high-level functioning: maintaining attention, organization, and executive function. A deficiency of norepinephrine within this brain region can cause inattention, problems with organization, and/or impaired executive functioning (Silver 2022)
  - *The limbic system* regulates our emotions. A deficiency in this region might result in restlessness, inattention, or emotional volatility (Silver 2022)
  - *The basal ganglia*—neural circuits that regulate communication within the brain. Information from all brain regions enters here and is relayed to the correct sites in the brain. A deficiency can cause information to "short-circuit" and result in inattention or impulsivity (Silver 2022)

- *The reticular activating system* is the primary relay system among the pathways that enter and leave the brain. A deficiency here can cause inattention, impulsivity, or hyperactivity (Silver 2022).

This provides some of the "why" behind the symptoms you experience as someone with ADHD.

Ok, that may be more science than even my fellow nerds are interested in, so I will not risk boring you any further. I highlight this research to remind you that you are not lazy. You are not unintelligent. You are not broken. Your brain does not work the same as someone without ADHD, but that is not a bad thing. You are capable of incredible things when you know how to use your brain to your advantage.

Textbooks and tall tales

When you think of ADHD, does an image of the little boy bouncing off the walls in school pop into your head? No surprise there; many people believe this is the only way ADHD presents itself. This could not be further from the truth. ADHD is currently categorized into three different types, with a lengthy list of presenting symptoms and many variations of those presentations from person to person. ADHD does not fit into a box, and neither do you.

In order to reach your goals, it is critical for those with ADHD—and the people we interact with—to understand that there are many other ways that ADHD presents in addition to physical hyperactivity. Knowing the broad spectrum of symptoms will help you evaluate your own experiences if you are uncertain whether you have ADHD.

Based on the most current (at the time of this writing) *Diagnostic and Statistical Manual of Mental Disorders* (2013), now in its fifth edition (known as *DSM-5*), there are three types of ADHD:

1. ADHD predominantly inattentive presentation
2. ADHD predominantly hyperactive-impulsive presentation
3. ADHD combined presentation.

With the predominantly inattentive presentation, you're going to see symptoms such as:

- fails to give close attention to details or makes careless mistakes
- has difficulty sustaining attention
- does not appear to listen
- struggles to follow through with instructions
- has difficulty with organization
- avoids or dislikes tasks requiring sustained mental effort
- loses things
- is easily distracted
- is forgetful in daily activities.

In the predominantly hyperactive-impulsive presentation, you will see symptoms such as:

- fidgets with hands or feet, or squirms in a chair
- has difficulty remaining seated

- runs about or climbs excessively in children; extreme restlessness in adults
- difficulty engaging in activities quietly
- acts as if driven by a motor in children; adults will often feel inside as if an engine is driving them
- talks excessively
- blurts out answers before questions have been completed
- difficulty waiting or taking turns
- interrupts or intrudes upon others.

And as its name might suggest, in the ADHD combined presentation:

- the individual meets the criteria for both inattentive and hyperactive-impulsive ADHD presentations (American Psychological Association 2013).

According to Johns Hopkins Medicine, combined (which is my diagnosis, in case you're curious) is the most common. While hyperactive/impulsive gets the most 'attention' (no pun intended), it is actually the least common. We have three presentations with defined criteria, but even within the same diagnosed ADHD type, symptoms will vary from person to person. The severity of symptoms can range from mild to severe, and symptom severity and presentation may change throughout a person's life.

That's a lot to process, but this is where we take all that mind-melting information and show you what it looks like for you as a leader (about time, right?). Communication, sustaining performance long term, executive functioning, impulse control, and mental hyperactivity will all impact how you function in the workplace. I will now break down each one and how they impact you at work.

Communication

Let's talk about communication challenges and what you can do to start working on them. How you share your thoughts with others makes perfect sense to you (and maybe even to others with ADHD). However, to a neurotypical person, your thoughts will often appear disjointed in the extreme. In your mind, your stream of consciousness perfectly aligns with the point you are trying to make, but it can be challenging to follow for some. Most neurotypicals are linear thinkers. ADHDers, not so much.

Pause for a moment and think back to your last conversation with a group of people at work. Be honest, how often did you interrupt or speak over the other people you were talking to? Your brain moves so fast that you just blurt out your exciting ideas or input so you don't forget them. Can't wait another second. Have to say it right now. This is something that I am terrible at. I put a ton of conscious effort into not interrupting, but even still, there are times when I catch myself doing it. Think about how it makes you feel when someone else speaks over you. I can't stand it. It makes me feel like they don't value my opinion or respect me as a professional and only want to hear themselves talk. As leaders, we never want to make someone else feel like they are not valued or respected. Being self-aware of this tendency can go a long way in building rapport with your team. When you catch yourself doing it, don't underestimate the power of an apology in the moment.

Have you ever noticed how impatient you are when the person you're communicating with is not succinct? Ironic, considering I just shared how long-winded I can be. Nevertheless, I tend to become very irritable when this happens. In my head I'm screaming, "Oh my god, just get to the point already! I don't have time for this!!" And yet I think I could win the world record for the longest filibuster in the legislature if I had the opportunity. ADHD can make you a hypocrite if you let it. They say you have two ears and one mouth for a reason—you should listen at least twice as much as you speak. As a leader, your job is not always to have the best ideas; *it is to make sure the best ideas are heard.* With practice, you can become more succinct and less irritable with others when it is their turn for the floor. The first step is to be mindful.

Would you consider strong memory an important aspect of communication? For most neurotypical people, their working (or short-term) memory allows them to easily store important information and pull it back up when needed. Your ADHD brain? That is not one of your strengths. In the executive function section of this chapter, I'll elaborate on what working memory is and how it impacts you, but when it comes to communication, not being able to recall important details can give the impression that you are not an engaged listener, and no one likes having an inattentive audience. Let me give you an example of what my internal dialogue almost always looks like in lectures, presentations, or during important conversations:

Brain: "Gwen, this conversation is important. Pay attention."

Me: "You're 100 percent right. Ok, I got this. I'm dialed in and attentive. Let's do this" . . . *one minor trigger or distraction sets off a train of thought that leads me to fall down a mental rabbit hole without even realizing it*

Brain: "Gwen, focus! You just missed something important. You can't ask it to be repeated without embarrassing yourself because you were supposed to be listening from the start. You don't want them to think you don't care what they're saying, do you?"

Me: "Crap. Yes. You're right. Ok, I'm back. I'm here. We're good. We're listening." . . . *the bullet-train brain carries me a million miles away from the boardroom before I even know I'm gone*

Brain: "Gwen! WE JUST TALKED ABOUT THIS!!"

Me: "Son of a ——!"

And on it goes.

When you become distracted, do you tell yourself, "I just need to try harder to focus"? When you have ADHD, distraction is not a conscious choice or the result of carelessness. It is due to brain wiring. Science—not an excuse, but an explanation. There is more to come on improving your focus and gaining better control of your wandering thoughts, but never forget you are not a bad person or a bad professional. You just need the right tools to succeed.

Reflect on your experience:

- Have others perceived you as rude or even bitchy because you often interrupt or talk over them in conversation?
- Have you ever been so excited about a thought you have during a conversation that you start to tune the other person out? You're waiting for them to stop speaking so you can share this exciting insight, but you have now lost everything they said while trying to hold onto that one thought.
- How often do you start speaking enthusiastically but become so sidetracked during your conversation that you cannot recall your original point and have to ask the other person what you were talking about?
- Do you sometimes feel like you lose your audience's engagement because they struggle to follow your train of thought, even though it makes sense to you?

If this sounds like you, do not be discouraged. Start with the tips I've provided throughout this section to improve in your target areas. Great leaders are great communicators; you will need to know your strengths and weaknesses in this area in order to progress.

In it for the long haul

Communication aside, have you ever felt like you're in a nosedive as a leader? How is it possible for things to start so well and end in a shit show? I asked myself this because most of my roles have been this way. My career path has been all over the place, and that's not uncommon for people with ADHD. That search for novelty (i.e., the search for dopamine) means that when we start something new, we often excel early on. We are excited, hyperfocused, dialed in, and man, do we soar. Before long though, boredom may start to creep in. You may feel disengaged and sense that you're missing out on your chance to do great things.

"What if I missed the boat?"

"What if I missed my calling?"

"What if I never figure out what I'm supposed to be doing?"

"Why doesn't this feel exciting or enriching anymore?"

"I am always so excited going in, but that rarely lasts for the long haul."

Your energy, enthusiasm, ambition, and creativity make you an attractive candidate for many roles. I tend to interview very well, and most people are excited to work with me after the interview process. But, how long does their excitement last before my "passion and uniqueness" turn into "burdensome and too different"? In Chapter One, I illustrated some of the stories from the role that almost made me walk away from leadership for good. You have seen that the "long haul" has been pretty short for me.

Being unaware of how ADHD affects you can lead to many hurdles as you navigate your career path. In my youth, I thought I was lucky. I always knew that I wanted to be a nurse. Straightforward, right? Not quite. Take a look at my resume and you will note that I have been a roamer as a professional. I have never stayed in one role for longer than 2.5 years and have lived in multiple states in the US as I bounced around trying to find my "best fit".

My first goal was to be a midwife. I worked as a bedside nurse in a high-risk labor and delivery unit, pretty much straight out of college. After two years of butting heads with some of my peers and bosses, I packed up and hit the road as a travel nurse for a few years. I thought it would be a fun way to see the country and find my forever home. Plus, it was nice to be onto something new as soon as I got bored.

My plans shifted away from midwifery when I was unexpectedly offered my first nursing leadership role at 27. While I had never loved any previous bosses, that first management position showed me what it was like to work for a genuinely toxic boss—the first of a few. Two nurse manager roles and one director of nursing role later, I was burned out (read: fried to a crisp) and needed a fresh start. On a whim, I pivoted to being a clinical value analysis director in supply chain for hospitals (I did not even know that was a thing before I took the job). Six months after starting that role, I also took on a side gig as a nursing school professor because I love to teach. When I decided to move on from supply chain, I had no idea what to do next. Through an impulsive decision, I ended up on the industry side of healthcare, working as a clinical specialist for a company that serviced the maternity care space.

Whew. Did you catch all that? I hope you didn't blink, you'd miss three different job changes I've had. Add in the two master's programs to all of that, and I think it is fair to say I have been a veritable professional tumbleweed. After the excitement of the new wore off or when I started to feel like I didn't fit in, off I went. At the time of writing this book, I have lived in the same city for five years (but held four different roles during that time), and I still get the itch. That feeling in the back of my head that I need to be moving on to the next adventure. Only after my diagnosis did I realize this feeling is pretty common for people with ADHD.

You may already know research tells us that switching jobs is a great way to improve career growth and lifetime earning potential (Christian 2022). So with ADHD, when does it help and when does it hinder? Start by focusing on the catalyst for why you're looking for something new. Are you moving on because you have that unquenchable thirst for the next big thing? Because you are beginning to struggle to fit in or perform up to someone else's expectations? Or is it because you have reached your full potential in your current role and need to move in order to grow? You need to know what you're looking for before recognizing when you've found it.

For those of you shaking your heads and saying, "I have been at the same job for X years, and I don't have any of those issues," consider generational and societal norms, as well as differences in symptom presentation and severity, as a factor. Maybe you've forced yourself to mask more or just forge ahead even though you are miserable because that is what is expected of you. Or, on the positive side, you may have just the right balance of novelty and routine, challenge and rejuvenation, and development and support—the perfect setup to help you thrive within one role or at least within the same company. If that's the case, that's fantastic! What you've found is the goal for everyone with ADHD: their ideal career match. If that's not you yet, do not be discouraged. Your fit is out there.

Take some time to reflect on your professional path. What are the patterns that you notice? What needs have you become aware of based on your past experiences? Evaluate how your current role compares to what you envision as your ideal role. Are you on a path that will take you to that ideal? Are you frustrated and reaching a point of burnout from feeling like it's only a matter of time before things go wrong? You are in good company here.

In Chapter Five and beyond, I will talk about the importance of finding your fit and what a game changer that can be. In the meantime, I'm going to give you a little more "why" behind your professional M.O.

Executive functioning—how you get stuff done

Executive functioning is defined as the cognitive process that organizes thoughts and activities, prioritizes tasks, manages time efficiently, and makes decisions (Barkley 2022). These abilities not only direct actions, they also control behavior and motivate us to achieve our goals and prepare us for future events. With ADHD, executive functioning challenges are the norm. Your "get up and go" seems to have often "got up and went", but it didn't bring you along for the ride. Let's tease out some of the components of executive functioning, so you know how to recognize them.

Do you live in a perpetual state of feeling overwhelmed? You may feel this way when faced with even a small task or responsibility, and it often makes no sense to neurotypical people or even yourself. I look at it like this: what might seem small to others can be the straw that breaks the camel's back for me. Why? Well, with my ADHD brain, I'm carrying around a lot *all the time.* My brain is always working a million miles a minute. Whether to productive ends or not, it just never stops. When you have this level of cognitive hyperactivity (AKA your brain is stuck in overdrive), something that appears to be small to someone else can be crippling and overwhelming to you. Your mental pot is always simmering, and adding even a tiny bit more heat can make it boil over. This concept makes sense when you've experienced it, but it is often very hard for neurotypical people to understand. They can get things done without being overwhelmed, so why can't we? Because we are not made the same way. You may have an excellent sense of direction, but if someone asks you to guide them somewhere in a language you do not speak, you will have a much harder time getting them where they want to go. Not because you are any less capable or knowledgeable but because you're not working on common ground.

If I tell you that I have to fight with my brain to initiate each and every task I undertake, does that sound familiar? Task initiation feels like trying to run a marathon through molasses. Whether it's a task that you are excited to do, dread the idea of doing, *have* to do, etc., it doesn't matter. Chances are, you will still feel stuck. Picture this: you are sitting in your office and your brain reminds you to check your email because that inbox is filling up fast. You know most of it is just FYI messages, so it shouldn't take that long to get through the actionable ones. So, you open your email and get to it, right? Nope. You sit there. Or maybe you decide now is a good time to water your office plant. Your brain starts becoming more insistent. You continue shifting things around on your desk, filing random paperwork, and cleaning your dry-erase board. On the outside, you may appear calm, but inside, you're anxious or even panicky. Your brain is screaming now, but your inbox remains closed. Why? You have *no* idea. You would feel so much better just getting it done, but you don't. This is called task paralysis. The anxiety associated with task initiation becomes so profound that you are trapped in doing nothing at all.

"Ok, but what about those beautiful moments where we've at last reached the point where we *do* start the task? We will be efficient, right? Leaders need to be great at that!" This is true, but ADHD leaders struggle to maintain focus even after overcoming task paralysis. For example, you intend to balance the upcoming schedule for your direct reports so you can send it to the team. You pull up the file on your computer but realize you're thirsty and think, "You know what? This is going to take a while. Let me grab some water." You go into the breakroom, open the fridge and grab a bottle. As you are about to walk back to your office, Tara, one of your team members, comes in and asks you about a project you tasked her to take the lead on. The paperwork she needs to get started is over in Victoria's office. You walk Tara to Victoria's office and give her the needed paperwork. Still, Victoria needs your help with a new hire onboarding plan before you leave. You help her get that all sorted out and are excited about the plan you two were able to create, so you head back to your office. When you sit down at your desk, your throat feels dry, and it dawns on you that you left your water bottle in the breakroom, so off you go to retrieve it. Before you know it, four hours have passed, and you have to leave because your dogs have an appointment at the vet that you've already had to reschedule twice. The schedule remains unbalanced, and the cycle starts all over again tomorrow. One hundred half-finished tasks because focus is not our forte.

Be honest; did you skim that story because you couldn't stay focused enough to read it in detail? Don't worry, I wrote it and did the same thing when completing the initial edit.

Remember a few sections back when I said I would come back to working memory? The irony of that question is not lost on me. ADHD brains have notable impairments in this arena. Working memory refers to thoughts or information you hold onto temporarily (short-term memory) so they're available to you when you need to pull them back up and complete a task.

In her article "Improve Working Memory: Brain Training Tricks" for *ADDitude* magazine (2022), Eileen Bailey describes it like this: "Think of working memory as a shelf in your brain. Imagine you are going to the store. You need milk, eggs, and bread. While you're in the store, you suddenly remember that you need cereal. You head to the cereal aisle, but as you focus on Special K, the eggs fall off your mental shelf. You arrive home with cereal, milk, and bread, but you have forgotten the eggs."

Many with ADHD experience significant struggles with working memory in all facets of life—not just in situations like the grocery store but also at work. In hallway conversations, impromptu meetings, or on-the-go phone calls, you will often lack the ability to write things down or to take notes. You think, "it's ok;

I know I will remember this", but chances are, you won't. Despite your best efforts, important information may just fly right out of your brain. It can be frustrating when you feel like you can't get it back, no matter how hard you try (I would be much less anxious if everyone in the world wore name tags because I can NEVER remember anyone's name despite them telling me 0.5 seconds ago or for the 50th time). If you struggle to remember important details, it can lead to missing deadlines, unmet expectations, and incomplete work.

When you are an executive, you need effective executive functioning skills, right? Well, duh. Actually, that is not where the term really comes from, but it's an appropriate correlation. Knowing how ADHD impacts your executive functioning abilities is the first step in ensuring these challenges do not get the best of you. We will cover how to turn that knowledge into action in Chapter Eight.

Assess if executive functioning challenges impact your daily life by taking this short quiz. Every yes is worth one point.

1. Do you often leave emails, voicemails, and text messages unaddressed because you feel overwhelmed?
2. Do you sometimes just sit and stare at your to-do list, unable to check off even one thing?
3. Do you often forget important details you swore you wouldn't have to write down in order to remember?
4. Do you have anxiety or panic attacks related to completing tasks, even small ones, but are still unable to get them done, no matter how anxious or panicky you feel?

5. Does the idea of taking on anything with multiple steps, like meal prepping or doing laundry, seem so Herculean that you avoid it until it becomes a near crisis?
6. Do you often procrastinate on things like paying bills, canceling unused subscriptions or memberships, making appointments, or submitting assignments?

This quiz is in no way an official diagnostic tool or a medical assessment. There's no official scoring system based on your answers. It's meant to make you think about how often ADHD appears in your day. When I reflected on my life and work after my diagnosis, I realized that there is no part of my life that ADHD doesn't touch.

Impulse control

ADHDers are IMPULSIVE, which can be a blessing and a curse. You might struggle with your finances, your performance at work, or ability to hold a job, and the overall successes of your life can be a direct result of unchecked impulsive behavior.

You now know that ADHDers are dopamine seekers, and you know why. We are always looking for ways to boost this neuro-chemical, as we have a lower baseline than our neurotypical peers. Seeking dopamine often goes hand in hand with impulsive behavior. We do what feels good. Spending money in excess (I swear Amazon Prime is the devil incarnate), making rash decisions without fore-thought, speaking without caring about the consequences of what comes out of your mouth, overcommitting to more than you can effectively manage, and failing to see the big picture because you are focused only on how good you feel in that moment. We are not hedonists; we just want our brains to be happy.

Once upon a time, I dropped multiple f-bombs in a room full of hospital leadership because someone was running late. Want to hear that story? Of course you do; everyone loves a good train wreck. In my first director role (yeah, that job again), I had a fantastic manager, Crystal Martinez, reporting to me. She was my perfect balance (we often called ourselves Maverick and Goose). Crystal tried her hardest to keep me reeled in (the girl deserves a medal because it is NOT an easy feat). She developed a trigger word to minimize the negative impacts of my impulsivity. If I were starting to get out of line in meetings, she would say "banana" to signal that I was rash in my communication or behavior and needed to tone it down.

Toward the end of that role, when I felt pretty awful about myself and my leadership abilities, Crystal and I were scheduled to attend mandatory leadership training along with numerous other leaders. I can't even recall what it was about, to be honest. Still, I didn't see the point of everyone being pulled away from their responsibilities for a session that I viewed as inconsequential. We arrived a few minutes early and found seats in a room full of supervisors, managers, and directors from across the hospital. We waited for a while, but the trainer did not show up. A few people tried to contact her and figure out if she was on her way, but I was getting irritated and impatient because "my time is important to me, and I have a lot of other things to do".

Impulsive (and awful) things started flying out of my mouth.

"This is f*cking ridiculous."

"What a waste of time."

"I have better things to do than to wait on this woman."

I was acting like an ass.

Poor Crystal tried her hardest to put the brakes on my demolition derby. She dropped the trigger word multiple times and even resorted to using my full name, "Gwendolyn Elizabeth!" But it didn't help. I continued to mouth off. The painful irony was that the whole time I was behaving this way, I *knew* it was inappropriate. In my head, I was telling myself to stop, but I couldn't. I don't know why I kept going and hated myself for it.

That is a small and personal example. Cringe-worthy, to be sure, and problematic in the big picture as it illustrates a pattern of harmful behavior. Our impulsiveness can also drive our coping mechanisms of choice. When ADHD remains undiagnosed or untreated, it is common for people to self-medicate with alcohol and substances that provide the dopamine spike or as a way to numb their feelings and slow down their thoughts. Adults with ADHD have an almost threefold risk of developing problems with substance abuse and addiction compared to neurotypical adults (SAMHSA 2015). When severe symptoms are unmanaged, the outcomes can be catastrophic. Does it surprise you to know that there is a tenfold increase in the prevalence of ADHD within adult prison populations compared to the general population (Young et al. 2014)?

If you have gotten far enough in your career that you hold a leadership position, or aspire to hold one, you may have put fail-safes into place to help mitigate your impulsivity at work and at home. For example, working with a financial advisor to pull money out of your bank account every month so that you never see it and can't spend it. Instead, you have it direct-deposited into a retirement account or an investment fund (I do this because I am horrendous with money). Maybe you set up a trigger word with a trusted colleague to try and keep you from saying things you will regret. These tactics act like rumble strips on the side of the road, keeping us within a safe zone and preventing impulsivity from causing us to crash and burn.

I have to be fair and point out that impulsivity sometimes works out well. Think about that time you hopped a last-minute plane to anywhere and had the best vacation of your life. Maybe you decided on a whim to quit your job to become an entrepreneur, and now you run a successful company. Good for you. Being impulsive has its upsides. The role I was in at the time of writing this book came as the result of a recruiter reaching out about a job I had no interest in taking. In that moment, I thought, "F*ck it, let's hear what he has to say." Within two weeks of that initial conversation, I had accepted the role. It came with a higher salary than I had ever achieved before and the flexibility to have the work/life balance I desperately needed. The key takeaway is that you need to mitigate the risks associated with being impulsive. It is not all good or all bad, but it does require balance.

Evaluate areas of your life where impulsivity may be harming you—excessive spending, lack of filter, short-term thinking with no plan for the future—instead of areas where it's helping you—signing up for a last-minute class to learn a new language, hiring a book coach (Kath Walters is second to none), or taking that new job that's way out of your comfort zone.

The big one: hyperactivity

When your brain moves fast, your body can struggle to keep up with it. The hyperactivity in ADHD is not just physical; it is many parts mental. Just because you cannot see the racing thoughts of cognitive hyperactivity—your brain going at a million miles a minute—doesn't mean you do not experience the physical impact. You might always feel tired, no matter how much sleep you get. How often do you catch yourself holding tension in your jaw and your face when trying hard to stay focused or even when you're zoned out and lost in thought? This can lead to headaches and muscle soreness. You may suffer from persistent full-body tension and fatigue from trying to slow down your bullet-train brain. I experienced extreme fatigue for years and spoke to multiple doctors attempting to get some answers. Still, no one could figure out the source of this exhaustion until I was diagnosed with ADHD.

Slowing your brain down to give your body a break is a double-edged sword because you often feel like you have to work even harder to apply the brakes. Traditional relaxation tools like meditation or sitting in silence are harder to adopt because the level of noise inside our heads is incredible and challenging to control.

Instead of trying to bring complete silence to your mind, practice sitting with yourself and allowing your thoughts to flow freely. Evaluate how that feels for you—not trying to control them, just letting them come. Sitting with a loud brain can cause notable discomfort and overwhelm at first. The inability to quiet your thoughts can be frustrating and defeating. Take a break when you need to. Be present enough to notice if intrusive and negative thoughts begin to take over. If allowing your brain to roam free makes you feel like you will spiral or you are overwhelmed with unhappy thoughts, consider doing this work with a trusted mental healthcare provider. They may be able to help guide you in a productive and cathartic processing of all the noise. Your brain has limitless potential. You are unlocking that potential by putting the work in to harness your strengths and build safeguards for your weaknesses. Throughout this book, I will continue to show you how.

📋 IN SUMMARY

We covered a massive amount of information in this chapter. If you've made it this far, take a break. Your brain and body need it. How did it feel reading the symptoms of each ADHD presentation? Have you found yourself in these pages?

Your ADHD brain can feel like a bullet train. You think faster and further than your neurotypical counterparts, so communication can be challenging. You may feel like every job starts well but ends in ruin, despite going in with your best intentions. The executive functioning challenges of "just getting it done" are much harder for you. Impulse control is a high-stakes game. While it has its upsides, there is a potential for significant negative impacts if not well controlled. It is common for your body to feel the effect of a brain always working overtime, and it's important to recognize when you need rest.

It will take time, but you must stop forcing yourself to function like a neurotypical person. Your neurodiversity is not your enemy. Instead, learn everything you can about how your brain works and what makes it special. Identify the areas of life where ADHD may have negative impacts, so we know where to start putting up guardrails. But, the most important thing is to give yourself grace.

Until now, we've been focusing on the brain, but what about the heart? The connections between these two vital organs run deep. In the next chapter, we will talk about ADHD and emotions. I will introduce you to rejection sensitivity dysphoria (RSD) and talk about how it impacts you as a leader, as well as covering the ways that ADHD influences your ability to connect with other people.

3

Bleeding Heart

Introduction

Emotional components and expressions of ADHD are not included within the current *DSM-5* diagnostic criteria. However, many researchers have acknowledged and accepted that these emotional expressions are an important part of ADHD. Certified ADHD coach, best-selling author, advocate, and founder of ADHD Works, Leanne Maskell, has even lobbied World Health Organization directors for the inclusion of emotional symptoms in the diagnostic criteria. I am hopeful that advocacy and research will come together to allow for emotional symptoms to be a part of the official diagnostic criteria in the future. In the meantime, I want to make sure you know how emotions and ADHD are tied together and how they impact your life and your work.

When I was 19 years old, I sat in front of my primary care provider sobbing, telling her I was concerned that I had undiagnosed bipolar disorder and wanted help to get an evaluation. At the time,

I thought that was the answer to my many emotional ups and downs. It was frightening to have such drastic changes in mood, often without explanation. I clearly made her very uncomfortable in this appointment, and she responded by saying she was not equipped to make that determination and provide a diagnosis. Fair enough. So I was sent to a therapist. At first, the therapist diagnosed me with borderline personality disorder, but later in my treatment, rescinded that diagnosis. I was left even more confused and unable to pinpoint these emotional shifts as being related to ADHD because no one else had made the connection. I had no idea that ADHD presented this way.

Tying this back to work, the tumultuous and often uncontrollable shifting of your mood in professional settings can be hard to understand for those around you. These mood shifts can be detrimental to your career as a leader. You may give off the impression of having unstable or unpredictable emotions and gain a reputation for being hot-headed or too emotional. By understanding how ADHD plays a role in your moods, you gain the power to work on controlling them more effectively. You can identify triggers and work to minimize emotional outbursts. It can also help you feel more confident in educating the people you work with about your ADHD, so they better understand the "why" behind the behavior. Not to be used as an excuse but as a chance for greater empathy while you work to build effective support systems for your emotions.

This is what undiagnosed ADHD can look like in the workplace. For example, I once broke down sobbing in an executive leadership meeting where it was announced that one of our peers had been let go. Upon hearing the news, I went into a rapid downward spiral because, in my head, I felt like this person was the ideal leader. If she wasn't safe from termination without warning, what did that mean for me when I was *far* from perfect? I tried to explain why I was so upset in a way that made sense to the other directors and executive team members, but they all looked at me like I was crazy or like I had some incurable disease that they did not want to catch. That emotional display was held against me in the counseling I later received concerning my ability to perform as a leader. If I had understood then how ADHD impacts my emotions, I might have been better prepared to handle this unexpected news. At the very least, I could have better articulated what was happening in my head to cause this reaction.

In this chapter, we will talk about the strong empathy and deep emotions tied to ADHD. Your emotional capacity can seem so much more profound than those around you. You may experience emotional instability, explosive anger, and come across as defensive or combative. We will cover the phenomenon of rejection sensitivity dysphoria (RSD), what it is and what it looks like when rejection becomes ruinous. I will share how it can seem like an impossible challenge to connect with other people. Between the chaos in your brain and the unpredictability of your emotions, you may be tempted to use self-isolation as a method of self-preservation. Finding the right connections can make all the difference. We will also touch briefly on romantic relationship challenges. This aspect of ADHD could fill an entire book on its own—and maybe I'll write that one next—but it is an important part of your journey to reach your full potential, so I will address it in that context at the end of this chapter.

Big feelings

Your experience and expression of the full spectrum of emotion can often feel so much more profound for you than for your neuro-typical counterparts. At the time of this writing, my nephew is seven years old. After a challenging day where he struggled to articulate himself well when frustrated, I could tell he needed support. I waited until he was ready to talk and asked him if he could verbalize what he had gone through on an internal level. "How do you think today went? What was going on in your head when you were frustrated?" He responded, "Auntie, I just have such big feelings, and I don't know what to do or how to talk about them." I tell you, my whole heart broke . . .

With ADHD, you feel big and you express big. Unfortunately, not everyone is comfortable with that. Though times are changing; there is a lot of evidence to support emotional expression in the workplace and showing up as your whole self. This is positive progress, but I have found very few professional environments that helped me express my emotions authentically to my ADHD brain. Your ideas, expertise, and insight can be lost in a sea of emotional expression that overpowers your messages. The extent to which you are underestimated can be significant. You may have your true potential ignored or maybe never unearthed at all.

In this same vein, ADHDers can often struggle to advocate for themselves without becoming defensive or aggressive for several reasons. You can overcommit to projects or responsibilities, but you do not want to let people down when you realize you're in over your head. You struggle to delegate or communicate when you've bitten off more than you can chew. RSD (coming up in the next section) might keep you from speaking up for yourself because you're worried about being rejected. Maybe you find the courage to speak, but you've held it in for so long that you end up lashing out in anger or frustration when you let it all out. These behaviors cause your primary message to be lost or diluted. Others will focus on how you behaved, not your intended message, and your attempt to advocate for yourself just made everyone doubt your capabilities.

The pot of water at a simmer example I used earlier to describe being mentally overwhelmed also applies to your emotional state, always on the cusp of boiling. At some point, the pot is destined to boil over, and you will have lost the ability to voice your feelings or concerns productively. You can come across as aggressive or hostile, and both are undesirable traits for any leader. At that point, you're not a leader; you're just another toxic boss.

A 2022 study by Babette Jakobi (a PhD candidate from Radboud University Medical Center in the Netherlands) et al. tells us that despite not being part of the core diagnostic criteria for ADHD, emotional dysregulation is a highly prevalent and clinically important component of adult ADHD. Up to 70 percent of adults with ADHD have symptoms of emotional dysregulation (Jakobi et al. 2022).

Do you sometimes feel the opposite of emotional? That level of numbness that makes you feel almost like a zombie? Dulled or absent emotions can be a coping mechanism, the result of masking, or the outcome of some medications used to treat emotional dysregulation. Think of it almost like a reset button. Your body and brain can only take so much emotional flooding before they have to shut down to protect themselves. This can be a compensatory mechanism after experiencing and expressing so much emotion, good or bad, all at once. It is not uncommon for adults with ADHD to feel these emotional peaks and valleys.

Do you ever find it challenging to articulate how you are feeling or explain how those feelings cause you to behave and communicate the way that you do, like my nephew that day? Do you feel your emotions are bigger and stronger than those around you, and you're not sure why? If you answered yes to these questions, that is the first step toward awareness of how ADHD impacts your emotions. In Chapters Eight and Nine, I will share tips and tools for putting your emotions to work for you as a leader.

You have spent many years masking your emotions. It can be difficult and frightening to bring them to the surface to find healthy, productive ways to process them. You may have never experienced psychological safety where it was okay just to "let it all out", so you may not feel comfortable doing so. I struggled with this a lot. There are still very few people I can let it all out in front of and not feel ashamed. This is a symptom of RSD. When I am alone, it can be cathartic to cry, scream, or sing at the top of my lungs to music that resonates with my feelings. Whenever possible, I make sure to do these things in a safe space, like on my couch with my dogs, in my truck, or on the phone with a trusted friend. I know it is easier said than done, but try to avoid these more extreme displays in public workspaces. They can lead to you being perceived in a negative light.

Sometimes the first step is to stop shaming yourself for how you express unfiltered emotions. Acceptance can often yield the greatest growth because you see yourself as worthy instead of shameful. You can work toward being your "best self" instead of beating yourself up for not being like everyone else.

Rejection sensitivity dysphoria (RSD)

I was blown away when I learned about rejection sensitivity dysphoria (RSD) because it explained so much of my behavior. According to the Cleveland Clinic (2022), RSD is when you experience severe emotional pain due to failure or rejection. There are many questions about causation or correlation here in how ADHD leads to the phenomena of RSD. Remember, people with ADHD receive 20,000 more negative messages by the ages of 10 to 12 than neurotypical people. It is unknown whether RSD is the brain's trauma response to this increase in negative messages during these formative years or whether it directly relates to the differences in brain chemistry associated with ADHD.

When completing research for this book, I interviewed Brooke Schnittman MA, BCC, PCC, an International Coaching Federation (ICF) and board-certified life coach and public speaker specializing in ADHD and executive functioning. She is the founder of Coaching with Brooke. Brooke shared that she was not officially diagnosed with ADHD until age 35. She feels that a lot of trauma from bullying could have been avoided had she known more about how her brain works. Brooke was bullied not only as a child but in her professional career because she was often "too honest, vulnerable, and prone to oversharing". Certainly an experience I can relate to. Can you?

It is possible to experience RSD in situations where rejection is only perceived instead of actual. I'll give you an example from one of my early sessions with my book coach, Kath. On that call, she asked me if it would be all right to speak to one of her friends in publishing to see if the concept of this book would be something a publisher might be interested in. Of course, I was excited that she was going to have that conversation with her friend, but also nervous and anxious to hear what the feedback was going to be. I hadn't even started writing earnestly, as we were still in the concept and outline phase.

When I met with Kath for our next session, I explained that I had been ruminating and anxious all week. I had been experiencing extreme self-doubt because I was worried about what this publisher would say about my idea. Kath was empathetic to my anxiety and said my self-doubt was normal for both new and experienced authors. Still, I did not hear her say anything further about the publisher's feedback. We moved on to discuss content, and in the throes of RSD, my negative and self-deprecating thoughts spiraled out of control.

"Oh no, Kath didn't say anything about the feedback from the publisher."

"She's trying to spare my feelings because she doesn't want to tell me it will suck and no one will want to read it."

"I knew it. I should give up. I will never be an author. I was so stupid even to think I could do it."

There was such a poisonous, internalized sense of not being good enough on a scale unreasonable to even the *potential* of this rejection. It was debilitating and devastating. The tragic and ironic part? The publisher said she thought my idea had potential, but I have no recollection of hearing Kath tell me that. I spiraled because of my perception of rejection, even though that was not the reality. This *is* the reality of RSD.

The effect is like tipping over dominos. Your fear of rejection can exacerbate your desire for perfection and cause even more mental and emotional overwhelm. It can also lead you to worst-case-scenario thinking and reinforce feelings of self-doubt, imposter syndrome, and low self-esteem. These can hinder your ability to perform at your best drastically. How difficult will it be for those around you to believe in your leadership abilities if you do not believe in them yourself?

What can it look like at work? In one of my later roles in the healthcare industry, I entered the company as a frontline employee reporting to the CEO. This company was a startup, so the organizational chart was almost flat. This indicated to me that there would be room for growth as the company expanded. At the time of my hire, I expressed that my goal was to be considered for leadership roles as those positions became available. Within less than two months of being hired, one of the company's VPs told me that I was clearly establishing myself as a leader within our clinical team and to keep up the good work. Fast forward a few months, and the first leadership position opened. It was not posted for applications, and no one was informed of the position being available . . . other than my colleague, who was the direct selection of our CEO for the role.

I was crushed. With my passion for leadership and personal development, my experience as a leader, and my education, I didn't know what else I could have done to prepare for the next step. Unfortunately, our leaders didn't see me that way, and I couldn't understand why. Cue the spiral. I was now reporting to the woman who was asked to take this position and my brain told me she would convince everyone that I was inept and I would lose my job. There was no merit to this thought process, just my bullet-train brain going off the rails. The tension between us mounted until she did the mature thing and asked to speak with me about how we would navigate this new dynamic.

The conversation started well; it was honest and productive. As we dug deeper into why I had such a hard time adjusting to her promotion, I broke down in the hotel lobby where we were meeting. I was sobbing so hard that the poor front desk attendant brought me over a box of tissues (sweet man). I told my new boss that I was petrified she would try to get me fired because we had struggled to get along, and now she was responsible for reporting on my performance. Why wouldn't she take the opportunity to send me packing? She hated me, right?

She looked right at me and said, "You see how extreme of a jump that is to make, don't you? From thinking that I don't like you to automatically thinking I'm going to get you fired?" From a logical and rational standpoint, she was 1,000 percent right, but RSD is neither logical nor rational.

You might be thinking, "I haven't seen this manifest in my work. I can take rejection with a grain of salt and keep moving forward without it stopping my momentum." This is great to hear, but bear in mind that RSD does not always or only show up at work. Sometimes it can be triggered by situations in your personal life with friends, family, and romantic partners. For some, it is only triggered by very specific scenarios. Like all ADHD symptoms, it can show up in unique ways for everyone.

Some people with ADHD might not experience RSD at all. For me, it has been a significant part of my presentation, and I know how life-altering it can be. The impact it has had on my leadership journey and professional life as a whole cannot be over-stated. You saw it in the story earlier, where I broke down crying over my colleague being let go, and you see two other snapshots of it here. Have you experienced anything similar?

Read the questions below and respond on a scale of 1 to 5, with 1 being unaffected by this/doesn't happen often, and 5 being devastating/occurs all the time.

1. When you experience rejection, whether direct or perceived, how does it make you feel?
2. Do other people seem to let things go when you can't seem to move past them?
3. Do things that roll off your colleagues' backs seem to wound you on a deeper level?
4. Does it take you much longer than others to "get over" rejection?

Looking at your score, does it illustrate that RSD impacts you in a significant way? If so, this is something that you will need to address when building your leadership skills. You may feel like you have no control over how you respond to rejection, but in Chapter Nine, we will discuss methods for reducing the grip of RSD.

Connections with others and self-isolation

Building and nurturing connections with neurotypical people can come with many hurdles. You often have to mask and mold yourself to neurotypical norms to feel like you can effectively engage with others in the workplace. When you struggle to "keep up the act", it can appear to outsiders as further emotional or mental instability because you seem inconsistent in your behaviors or communication style. You may often overshare in an attempt to make a connection, leaving you feeling embarrassed or ostracized.

In extreme instances, your challenges in connecting with people can lead to self-isolation. When you feel that no one understands you and you are always "getting it wrong", you may retreat from others altogether. You experience exhaustion from trying so hard only to feel hurt by your inability to make the connections you crave (I have fallen into this category before).

Relationship building and networking are essential to the success of any leader. To establish rapport, you need to connect with colleagues, clients, investors, board members, executive leaders, and, of course, direct reports. If you cannot authentically make or maintain these connections, you will struggle to be effective as a leader, which can impact your ability to move up. We all know it's about who you know, and if you cannot make the right connections, you will miss out on professional opportunities.

In my first director role (and most of my life), I had a hard time connecting. I was the youngest of the hospital directors, over half of whom were of a different generation altogether. I was working insane hours, plus getting my first master's degree. Add in being an upstate New York native in a south Texas city (where my loud mouth and no-nonsense attitude were not the norms). You can imagine why I often felt stressed, out of place, and in over my head.

One day it became too much, and I snapped at one of the other leaders when I was told I was not meeting expectations. In addition to apologizing to that leader, I set up a meeting with our chief nursing officer to discuss my challenges and why I had behaved that way. I know the rules when communicating with executive leadership: BLUF (bottom line upfront). Keep it as short and sweet as possible. Instead, when I sat down in her office, I word-vomited most of my life story without thinking. I spoke of my emotional struggles and crippling self-doubt, which led to defensiveness. At this time, I did not know about my ADHD, so it was not discussed. When I stopped talking, she said, "But this isn't a new problem or situation. I thought you were going to tell me something recent and immediate in your personal life that you were struggling with that made you act this way." Yikes. In that instant, I knew I had said too much. I painted a picture of myself that, to her, not only didn't make sense, but set the stage for why that team came to believe I was incapable of being an effective leader.

You might think, "I have never had any issues connecting with people." Some people with ADHD have mastered the art of connecting with others because they have harnessed their emotional depth and breadth and used it to their advantage. Empathy is a strong foundation for connection and relationships, and ADHDers often have the ability to be more empathetic than their neurotypical peers. Positive connection is the goal that all ADHDers can attain with the right tools in place.

Are you someone who feels that they don't need to make real connections at work? That you're not there to make friends, you're just there to do your job? I have known people who can achieve success while maintaining this separation between work and their personal lives; it is not unheard of. But it is not the norm. Connections matter when you want to achieve big things and act on all of your big ideas. I am not someone that tries to keep others at a distance in the workplace. I crave connections with others, and it brings out the best in me as a leader when I feel genuine connections to my colleagues, direct reports and executive leadership. Neither approach is wrong, and intentional separation is ok. I only offer a word of caution because I have seen how powerful connections can be for successful ADHDers.

What happens when you reach that point I mentioned earlier: self-isolation? While isolation can feel like a method of self-preservation, it is important to remember that human beings are not designed to be solitary creatures. I am going to go deep here and say if you are struggling to find meaningful connections in your life, resulting in hopelessness, despair or suicidal ideation, please reach out to someone you trust. Lean on your friends, loved ones, partners and even healthcare providers during these times.

If none of these is a viable option for you, dialing 988 on your phone in the United States will connect you to the suicide and crisis hotline via phone call, text or even chat function. For readers in other countries, a quick Google search of crisis support hotlines can provide you with the most appropriate number to use where you live. Please know you are not alone and reach out for help if you have no one to turn to.

Ok, back to work stuff. Let's reflect again. How often do you avoid networking events or even regular conversations with your colleagues because you struggle to feel real connections with them? Have you caught yourself oversharing in an effort to make connections? Still, it does not ever seem to "land" the way you want it to, and you are often left feeling guilty or ashamed because you said too much. I will share with you a piece of advice my therapist says to me often: "Not everyone deserves what you have to offer." Let that sink in for a second.

There is nothing wrong with seeking connections. We've discussed why it is a huge component of a successful and fulfilling life. But do your best not to seek deep connections indiscriminately. Differentiate between the people in your life who deserve your deepest energy and those with whom you can be okay just having surface-level relationships. When you save your energy for people who reciprocate that energy, it will help prevent you from burning out or becoming disheartened from trying to connect on a deep level with people who will never meet you there.

Social anxiety can hinder your ability to seek and make connections with others, as can RSD or a traumatic past of not finding meaningful connections. You may be exhausted from trying and just want to give up. By getting to know yourself and your brain and working toward the best of both, you will attract the right kind of people to you who will be exactly what you need.

Romantic relationship challenges

I wanted to touch on romance because all of the emotional components of ADHD we have reviewed in this chapter can directly impact your ability to find and maintain a healthy romantic relationship. By healthy, I mean one that meets the needs of you and your partner, is built on trust and effective communication, and honors and supports your ADHD presentation.

A romantic relationship's stability, or lack thereof, can make or break you at work. As a leader with ADHD, you already struggle to maintain focus, retain important information, navigate emotional expressions professionally, and manage the millions of thoughts going through your head at any given time. The health of your relationships at home can help calm your storm or risk sinking your ship. Therefore, it is important not to neglect this aspect of your life when attempting to optimize your leadership performance.

Evidence shows us that having a supportive partner can minimize the negative impact of ADHD symptoms, which can help us achieve optimal performance at work. For example, in the 2021 study "Adult ADHD and Romantic Relationships: What We Know and What We Can Do to Help" by Wymbs et al., the authors reveal that 96 percent of spouses of adults with ADHD felt that their partner's symptoms interfered with their functioning in one or more domains such as organization, time management, and communication. Unmanaged ADHD can put a strain on relationships, and strained relationships can prevent you from achieving your goals.

You might be thinking, "I don't have a partner. Are you saying there's no hope for me to be successful?" Not at all. At the time of writing, I have been mostly single for six years. In that time, I finished two master's degrees, held multiple leadership roles, executed large and complex strategic projects on short timelines, became a college professor, started a bakery business, founded the END (Excellence in Neurodiversity) Institute, and wrote this book. I don't say any of that as a brag, just to provide reassurance that while it can sometimes be easier with a supportive partner, the lack of one is not a barrier to your success.

Having a strong sense of self-worth is important, and only you know what works best for you. If, however, your partner is making things difficult for you to achieve success at work, I will review some helpful tools in Chapter Nine that can help build a stronger relationship if you and your partner are willing and able. Remember, the goal is to have a partner to calm the storm instead of sinking the ship.

Think about your current situation and your romantic history. Have you struggled to find and maintain a healthy romantic relationship as an adult? Have you felt that the lack of a romantic partner has made it harder to maintain your optimal performance at work because the whole world rests on your shoulders alone? The more you know about how ADHD impacts you, the more authentic you can be in a relationship. If you have a partner, communication is everything. You must talk with them about your challenges and strengths, and ensure you both have the same expectations. If you are searching for a partner, make sure the people you allow into your life support you in the ways you need, based on your ADHD presentation. Communication is just as important here.

How can you be the best partners for one another based on your strengths and struggles? These are conversations you should have on a routine basis, not just one-and-done. You must check in often to ensure everyone is holding up their end of the bargain. When you are on the same page and everyone's needs are being met, it reduces the risk that relationship struggles will negatively impact you at work.

Along with executive functioning challenges and overall ADHD symptoms impacting your daily life, RSD and emotional dysregulation can present challenges in dating and long-term relationships. You may harbor a lot of doubts and fears about finding or keeping a partner that will support you in life and your career. You may have sworn off dating altogether. I fall into both of these boats, depending on the day. I do hope to find the right romantic partner to share my life with. Still, I have come to recognize that settling for anything less than the person perfect for me (because there is no such thing as universal perfection) robs me of the support and loving experience I deserve. I hope you love yourself enough to feel that way too.

I would love to hear about your experiences of how your partner has positively impacted your leadership journey. Join the END Institute groups on LinkedIn or Facebook and share your stories.

📋 IN SUMMARY

In this chapter, we learned that, while not included in the official diagnosis criteria, the emotional presentations of ADHD are a significant piece of the puzzle, with implications on performance and opportunity as a leader. How we experience and express emotions are different and not always appreciated or understood. RSD can be debilitating, causing crippling self-doubt and negative thinking. While we crave connections with others, we can often struggle with meaningful connections even though they are critical in leadership. Romantic relationships can help us when they're healthy and supportive or hinder us when they serve as another source of chaos or uncertainty.

You must stop shaming yourself for your emotions. Stop bottling them up, hiding them away or repressing them into oblivion. They will often come back with a vengeance, which will only hinder your career progression. Instead, start building awareness of any emotional dysregulation you might experience. Lean into your emotions, explore them and get to know them. Sometimes that will mean sobbing your eyes out or screaming at the top of your lungs. That is okay. Try to do these things in a space where it will not negatively reflect on you at work. Protect your energy and stop seeking deep connections with everyone indiscriminately; seek out the right types of people. If you have a romantic partner, start working with them on how your partnership can better optimize your professional performance.

We have covered a lot in this chapter, and it is possible that you may be feeling emotionally drained or overwhelmed with all of this. Take a break if you need to. This book isn't going anywhere.

When you're ready, in the next chapter, we are going to talk about ADHD diagnosis. If the content in these first three chapters resonated with you and you saw yourself on some of these pages, you may wonder, "How do I know for sure?" and "What do I do next?" If so, break into the next chapter, where we will dive into what diagnosis looks like and what it can mean for you.

4

The Big D

Introduction

Let's talk diagnosis. You may have already started to self-diagnose as you've read the first three chapters. That was intentional. The impact of diagnosis is different for everyone, whether you choose self-diagnosis or the formal process of clinical diagnosis. I want you to feel comfortable knowing that no matter which path you choose, you do not have to follow the medical model for managing your ADHD symptoms if you don't want to. Many people choose not to.

Diagnosis is liberating for many, myself included. My entire life made sense when I realized I had ADHD. After my nephew was diagnosed, his pediatrician told my sister that there is a genetic component to ADHD. It is estimated that around half of all children with ADHD have at least one parent with the condition. Right away, I started researching—not only for his benefit but to see if it was something my sister and I should also be evaluated for.

The more I learned about ADHD, the more apparent it became that my sister, mother, and I were also neurodiverse. Once I had enough information to correlate my life experiences to the diagnostic criteria, I chose to seek a clinical assessment. When the practitioner confirmed my diagnosis, it felt like I could see the world in focus for the first time. I processed it for a few days before deciding to tell the world. I announced it on all my social media accounts and, from then on, decided to post evidence-based information and my personal experiences with undiagnosed ADHD. In sharing my journey, I wanted to make it easier for others to identify if they might be in the same boat. Finding and understanding reputable sources of ADHD information can be overwhelming. My hope was to make learning about the condition stress-free and easy to access.

Enough about me. You want to seek a diagnosis. So what are your options?

There are two types of diagnosis:

1. Self-diagnosis, where you do your own research and determine, based on the diagnostic criteria, that you meet those criteria.

2. Clinical diagnosis, where you undergo an evaluation or assessment from a qualified medical professional and receive an official clinical diagnosis.

I will expand on both of these throughout the chapter and provide some additional helpful information you can use to seek a diagnosis. When deciding which diagnosis route to take, consider what it will mean for you and why you want one. Then, through diagnosis and understanding of your symptom management options, you can choose how to optimize your ADHD in a way that works for you.

"Isn't ADHD overdiagnosed these days?" Ah, so you've heard that, have you? We are going to set the record straight. Some people have raised concerns that there is a wave of overdiagnosis of ADHD because it is now "trendy", and everyone is talking about it. I am a nurse and love evidence, so in the 'Skepticism and bias' section of this chapter, I will use data to explain the rational rise in diagnosis, particularly among adults and women. You may feel frightened by the prospect of being diagnosed with a neurological condition. I will break down the process into more palatable pieces to make it less daunting. There is a lot of stigma surrounding mental health and neurodiversity, but that should not hold you back from reaching your full potential with the knowledge and tools you gain from a diagnosis.

The diagnostic process, and access to it, varies around the world. In some locations like the UK, the waiting list for an evaluation and clinical diagnosis via the National Health Service (NHS) can be years long. You may seek diagnosis through a private clinic, which can be much quicker than the NHS. Still, there are additional costs associated that may make this an unrealistic option. In the United States, you may seek a diagnosis from your primary care provider or a psychiatric mental health professional. I went to a psychiatric nurse practitioner.

It is a good idea to consider who is covered by your insurance, who is accepting new patients, and who specializes in adult ADHD in your area. Taking those things into account, I was left with just one option, but there may be multiple options for you depending on your location and financial resources.

Why seek diagnosis?
A diagnosis of ADHD—self- or clinical diagnosis—is the foundation for understanding your experiences and learning to optimize your symptoms.

With self-diagnosis, you have determined, based on your research and personal experience, that you fit the *DSM-5* diagnostic criteria. In this process, you may come across a multitude of screening tools, online assessments, checklists, etc. Make sure to research which of these resources is reputable before using it as a guide.

In clinical diagnosis, you are evaluated by a healthcare professional using diagnostic tools, such as questionnaires and feedback from your family and friends. These often include questions about symptom expression that goes all the way back to childhood. There is no blood test or routine imaging that can diagnose ADHD. It is all based on subjective and objective evaluation of symptoms. The diagnostic process and tools used will vary depending on the type of provider you go to seeking a diagnosis. Your primary care provider may use a shorter questionnaire because you have less time with them in a routine appointment. They may offer a diagnosis on the spot. A psychiatrist may use a longer evaluation tool and request feedback from your family, friends, and others who have known you since childhood. This can mean you may not get a diagnosis that day, as that information can take time to gather.

I want to be clear, I am not saying that either self-diagnosis or clinical diagnosis is better than the other. There are benefits to both. With self-diagnosis, you're not waiting to see a provider. A wealth of information is available from *reputable* sources that can help you conduct self-guided research. You may learn more on your own than you would from a primary care physician in a quick medical appointment. Still, you MUST use reliable sources (some of my favorites are listed at the back of the book). There's no cost associated with self-diagnosis other than the time you spend researching the condition, which can be done at your own pace.

Clinical diagnosis, however, provides an avenue for prescription medication if that is what you want. It may also make it easier to seek and receive specialized treatment. In the United States, you cannot receive prescription medication for ADHD treatment without a clinical diagnosis. Therefore, it is important to research which treatment options require a clinical diagnosis and which are available with self-diagnosis, as this can impact your decision-making process.

You might think providers are all pill pushers, and you will just be handed a prescription instead of having a collaborative conversation about your care. Before your clinical diagnostic appointment, reread this chapter, print out the chart in 'The link between diagnosis and management' section, and discuss your options with your provider. Together, come up with a collaborative plan that works for you.

If you have been searching for answers for a long time with little to no luck, you are probably frustrated. You may have even been misdiagnosed along the way, resulting in a mistrust of the medical community. I have been there, and I feel your frustrations.

So why bother? Because you deserve it.

You deserve an explanation for your experiences and an understanding of how your beautiful brain works. This allows you to manage and leverage your symptoms to your professional advantage. As I mentioned, when I received my diagnosis, it felt like a massive weight was lifted off my shoulders. At last, I had clarity when looking back on my experiences and struggles across my life and leadership journey. The emotional volatility, RSD, communication difficulties with some of my peers, perfectionism, a constant feeling of overwhelm, task paralysis, forgetfulness, etc., all screamed ADHD. There were my answers. I felt like I could take a deep breath for the first time in as long as I could remember.

After I shared my diagnosis and started talking about my experiences, it opened the door for incredible conversations with other ADHD professionals online. I was surprised to find that so many friends and colleagues I've known for quite a long time had ADHD—I had never known. Putting a name to your experiences can provide great relief and a roadmap for navigating your way through a successful leadership career.

You might be thinking, "I'm afraid to get a diagnosis. I do not want to be labeled." The choice is always up to you. The tools discussed later in this book can be valuable resources for leveraging your brain's superpowers for both clinical and self-diagnosis. Nothing requires me to disclose my diagnosis to anyone other than the people I choose. However, check your local regulations. With a clinical diagnosis of ADHD, are you required by law to disclose that to anyone? In many instances, the answer will be no. You can keep the information to yourself if that would make you feel more comfortable.

How does the possibility of a diagnosis make you feel? Have you felt lost because you never seem to get answers that make sense, or have you been given solutions that don't result in notable improvement? If you feel overwhelmed or scared, take a step back and consider how a diagnosis will impact you as an individual. Make an appointment with your primary care provider or therapist and discuss it with them to get their perspective on the diagnostic process. Do they think it will benefit you? When you are comfortable doing so, look into specialists in your area or get recommendations. Try to find providers that specialize in adult ADHD to ensure the person you are working with provides you with the most comprehensive information and resources about diagnosis and treatment options.

Cost and length of wait times for assessment can be prohibitive factors to seeking diagnosis. In the United States, try seeking a provider within your insurance network to reduce costs, so you are only responsible for the co-pay. Discuss diagnosis with your primary care provider if that is the most effective route. For example, my sister received her diagnosis from her primary care provider and had access to the same level of support and follow-up as I had with the psychiatric nurse practitioner who provided my assessment and diagnosis.

Depending on where you live and the availability of resources in your area, you may find assessment wait times unavoidable. Try looking into telemedicine or virtual appointments. This may allow you to see someone not in your immediate region who may have shorter wait times for evaluation appointments. Just remember to check with your insurance provider to ensure this is covered and you are not hit with an unexpected and expensive bill. We don't want to add another source of anxiety to the process.

The link between diagnosis and management

ADHD symptoms are managed in a plethora of ways. Your health-care team may suggest options, or you may come across treatments in your own research that you think might be a good fit for you. There is no single approach to treating ADHD, and it is important that you feel empowered to advocate for the options you are most comfortable with. I wanted to cover some basic information on commonly used treatments so you have an idea of some of your choices. This list is by no means exhaustive. Talk with your health-care provider or mental health professional about other possibilities.

Let's start with medications. At the time of writing this, two types of medications are being used to treat ADHD: stimulants and non-stimulants. Stimulants are considered first-line treatment and, at present, are the most common. Amphetamines like Adderall fall into this category, along with methylphenidate (e.g. Concerta® or Ritalin®). Non-stimulants are prescribed to patients who don't tolerate or see benefits from stimulant medications. Up to 30 percent of patients don't respond to stimulants.

Non-stimulants may also be prescribed alongside stimulants to treat the symptoms that the latter do not alleviate.

Therapy can be an effective tool in ADHD treatment. In particular, cognitive behavioral therapy (CBT) has been shown to improve ADHD symptoms. Mayo Clinic (2019) defines CBT as a common type of talk therapy or psychotherapy. It helps you become more aware of inaccurate or negative thinking, so you can view challenging situations more clearly and respond to them more effectively.

If medication or therapy are not your style, treatment can also come in the form of ADHD coaches and support groups. There are multiple levels of certification that a coach can receive specific to ADHD, and you may find coaching helpful if you have a difficult time navigating your diagnosis or you feel as though you are in a transitional period in your life. The ADHD coaches I have spoken with work so well because they help you address your sticking points or challenges in ways that align with your unique brain. I have met ADHD coaches specializing in everything from nutrition to fitness, entrepreneurship, female professionals, and students. More on this will come in Chapters Six and Seven, but I want to point out that not all coaching is the same. However, if you invest in it, having someone certified (or at least specialized) in ADHD coaching can make a world of difference.

There is no one size fits all treatment. Managing your symptoms is a personal journey, not in the sense that it will not impact others, but that you are the one living with this brain and will know what makes it function optimally. Regardless of how you choose to seek diagnosis, it is important to know all of your treatment options so you can explore your choices and figure out what makes the most sense for you.

At this point in my journey, I use a combination of medication and therapy as the foundational tools for managing my symptoms. I do not say this to advocate for or against medication, only to be honest. Because of this foundation, I can further build support systems and implement techniques to optimize my ADHD. Some of my support systems include physical exercise, grounding exercises, adapting my environment to support my needs, and ADHD coaching. I know many very successful people that have chosen to be unmedicated. However, I know many people who have found an equal measure of success but do not feel they can survive without meds, which is not an exaggeration. It is life or death for them to have that support. Some of the people I know are in therapy, and some are not. The path you walk will always be your own. I chose the clinical diagnosis route along with medication and therapy because that is what works best for me right now.

You may decline medication, but I strongly urge you not to decline all types of ADHD support and symptom management. To guide you on this journey, utilize other tools like exercise, therapy, support groups, coaching, etc. There is also nothing that says you have to stay on medication forever. Everyone responds in a unique way to ADHD meds. If you decide to try them out, you will talk to your provider regularly about how the medication impacts you and your symptoms. Then, you can explore other options or decide against medication altogether if it's not working. Choosing a treatment plan involves a lot of big decisions at once. Taking a patient and gentle approach with yourself is the key to successfully navigating and exploring your symptom management.

In the chart below, categorize five possible treatment options: medication, CBT, exercise, support groups, and coaching. In the column labeled 'Interest in', assign a number 1 through 5; 1 being no interest, 5 being very interested. In the column labeled 'Knowledge about', assign a number 1 through 5 again, but this time, 1 is no knowledge and 5 is very knowledgeable.

	Interest in	Knowledge about
Medication		
CBT		
Exercise		
Support groups		
Coaching		

Use this chart in conversations with your healthcare providers to help create your individualized treatment plan. It's a great, low-stress way to start a conversation. There's a digital copy for printout on my website if you would prefer something physical that you can bring into the appointment.

You might be afraid of losing autonomy and control over managing your symptoms. You might feel like you don't know enough to make the right decisions and worry that that means others will do it for you. Here I have given you some baseline information to start you off. You know a lot more than before you began this book. Trust your knowledge, and do not be afraid to advocate for yourself in the treatment planning process.

Roleplay

No, not that kind. We're focusing on diagnosis here; get your head out of the gutter! Ahem. Ok, back on track. The role that diagnosis plays in your life is up to you. Your diagnosis is not a straitjacket. It does not confine you to one course of treatment or any treatment at all, for that matter. You can choose to share your diagnostic information with the world or no one at all. It's up to you. Some people see diagnosis as a label or an excuse, but I challenge you to reframe it as a *concrete explanation*. What you do with that information is still your responsibility.

There is no one correct answer to what you do with your ADHD diagnosis if you seek one. When I was diagnosed and shared the revelation on social media, numerous people reached out to me who were adamant in directing me not to take medication. I read books on ADHD that demonized pharmaceutical treatment and the pharmaceutical industry at large and asserted that you would have a much better life without it. Everyone's a critic, right? However, I also know friends, acquaintances, and content creators that swear by the benefits of taking medication and call it life-changing. Everyone will have something different to say, but none of them are you, and that's the important part. Managing ADHD, like so many behavioral conditions, is a trial-and-error process of finding what combination of resources and tools work for you. There is no blueprint for success and no shortcuts. You will still need to put in the work to make your neurodivergent brain your greatest asset.

You might think, "If I receive a diagnosis, it will define me and limit me." A diagnosis does not have the power to do that; only you do. It will define you if you use it as an excuse for poor behavior or performance that you make no attempt to improve. It will limit you if you do not identify how to optimize your symptoms and instead allow them to hold you back

How does it feel to know the power rests in your hands? That you retain control over the course of your life and leadership potential regardless of a diagnosis? Are you empowered? Afraid? Overwhelmed? I have just laid a lot of responsibility at your feet, but I do not do so lightly. Chapters Seven, Eight, and Nine are all dedicated to *how* you can make ADHD work for you.

Skepticism and bias

There is skepticism and bias in some parts of the medical community and the world about overdiagnosis, but it is not based on truth. Some medical professionals and laypeople feel that ADHD is "trendy" right now, and providers are being lax in their diagnosis and treatment of the condition because it has been getting more attention from the general public in recent years.

The rise in diagnosis has much more to do with the increased understanding of the condition and how it presents through ongoing research, and almost nothing to do with being trendy. I'm not saying that there's a zero percent incidence of misdiagnosis. Always make sure that you are evaluated and diagnosed by a qualified medical professional if you choose a clinical diagnosis and use evidence-based tools if you choose self-diagnosis.

It might feel like skepticism is valid because it can even come from medical professionals. Allow me to present a fascinating case study as a reminder that even medical professionals are fallible. Grab the popcorn; this one is good.

In 1846, Hungarian physician Dr. Ignaz Semmelweis recognized that the patients in the maternity ward were dying at alarming rates in Vienna General Hospital, where he worked. After trying to identify the cause, he noted that in the student/doctor-run medical ward, patients had a much higher risk of fever and death than in the midwife-run maternity ward next door. The doctors and medical students often rounded on the ward directly after performing autopsies on cadavers, a task not performed by midwives. Dr. Semmelweis theorized that "cadaverous particles" were transmitted on the doctors' hands to the maternity patients and caused them to become ill (The Global Handwashing Partnership 2017). As a result of this theory, he implemented a mandatory handwashing protocol for doctors. Lo and behold, the mortality rates in the Vienna General medical maternity ward plummeted.

In 1850, he presented to the Vienna Medical Society about the benefits of handwashing. However, he was rejected and ostracized so severely that even Vienna General Hospital abandoned its handwashing requirement, despite evidence that his method was saving lives (The Global Handwashing Partnership 2017).

It was not until the 1870s that doctors began washing their hands routinely before surgeries. Later still, Louis Pasteur used

Semmelweis's work as a catalyst in his development of the germ theory (The Global Handwashing Partnership 2017). Finally, in the 1980s, hand hygiene was officially incorporated into American healthcare with the first national hand hygiene guidelines. It took us over 140 years to get that message. Still think healthcare providers know it all? Give me a moment to jump off my soapbox. Thank you for allowing me to nerd out about medical history just to prove a point.

Lack of in-depth understanding of the exact cause of ADHD has meant that many adults have gone into the professional world undiagnosed, not knowing how to use their brain wiring to their advantage, and struggling with the impact of their symptoms. Concerns of overdiagnosis may also cause some providers to hesitate in diagnosing their patients. So how common is ADHD? I don't think we will know the real answer to that for quite some time because so many individuals with ADHD remain undiagnosed.

These are the estimates we have available right now. Research by PhD student Melissa Vos and Dr. Catharina Hartman published in the *Journal of Global Health* (2022) states that, among the general population, prevalence estimates for ADHD range from 5 to 7 percent in childhood and 3 to 5 percent in adulthood. However, the study points out that much less research is available focusing on adult ADHD.

Interestingly, the publication states that a recent meta-analysis shows the prevalence of adult ADHD in those 50 years and older is far lower, with a measly diagnosis rate of 0.23 percent (Vos and Hartman 2022). These data points show that we have still not captured the true prevalence of adult ADHD, as evidenced by the steep drop in diagnosis rates among the 50+ population. This could be due to changes in the availability of research, generational differences, and shifting societal norms over the span of a lifetime. While some have claimed that ADHD goes away in adulthood and that overdiagnosis is rampant, I would argue that we just do not have the appropriate amount of research or in-depth understanding of the exact cause of ADHD to say with confidence that we have been accurate in our diagnosis of patients across the lifespan.

Our evolving understanding of this type of neurodiversity is helping give a name to the struggle that so many have suffered with in silence for their entire lives. This is confirmed by the article "ADHD Statistics: New ADD Facts and Research" in *ADDitude* magazine from July 2022, which states:

> *Adult ADHD diagnosis rates are rising. ADHD diagnoses among adults are growing four times faster than ADHD diagnoses among children in the United States. A 26.4% increase among children compared to 123.3% increase among adults. Still, ADHD is thought to be underdiagnosed in adults compared to children. Most scientists believe that adult ADHD remains underdiagnosed, because diagnostic criteria for ADHD in the DSM-5 were developed for children and because adults with ADHD often have comorbid psychiatric disorders that may mask the symptoms of ADHD. It is estimated that fewer than 20% of adults with ADHD are currently diagnosed and/or treated by psychiatrists (ADDitude Editors 2022).*

You may be asking, "How can so many more people have ADHD now than ever before?". My answer to that is, "They don't." ADHD is not new. The symptoms have been classified under many names, such as the disease of attention, simple hyperexcitability, abnormal defect of moral control, hyperkinetic reaction of childhood, and attention-deficit disorder or ADD (with or without hyperactivity). The presentations were often attributed to moral failings before it had a name. What we used to call behavioral problems and laziness, we now know in some cases, can be ADHD.

Children and Adults with Attention-Deficit/Hyperactivity Disorder (CHADD) is a national organization in the United States that was formed in 1987 to provide information, support, and advocacy for ADHD adults and parents of ADHD children. One of their routine publications is called *ADHD Weekly*, and in 2018 they published an article titled, "More Fire Than Water: A Short History of ADHD", in which the authors discuss how far back ADHD symptoms have shown up in recorded history.

The earliest mention of what seems to be ADHD was by Hippocrates, often called the father of modern medicine. He lived in Greece from about 460 to 375 BC. He was known to have made at least one reference to some patients who could not keep their focus on any one thing for long and had exceptionally quick reactions to things around them. He thought the cause was an "overbalance of fire over water." recommended a bland diet that included fish, but little other meat, a lot of water and lots of physical exercise (CHADD 2018).

While our knowledge of the causes of ADHD has grown quite a bit since then, I can relate to being a little more fire than water, can't you?

Are you concerned that you may be misdiagnosed if you seek an assessment? What might the implications of that look like for you? Refer back to the *DSM5* diagnostic criteria and reference material, such as this book and other reputable sources, to create a solid case for why you believe you have ADHD. This will reduce the risk of misdiagnosis. For example, I thought I had bipolar disorder and was misdiagnosed with borderline personality disorder because I did not understand how to articulate the full spectrum of my symptoms. With the information you have read here, you are armed with everything you need to speak with eloquence about your ADHD presentation and associated symptoms.

📋 IN SUMMARY

In this chapter, you have learned about the types of diagnosis and what you can do with that diagnosis. You now know there are many treatment options, and you are the one that's going to determine which is right for you.

I want you to stop fearing the stigma of diagnosis. If your symptoms are debilitating and you need help managing them, diagnosis is a great first step, whether you want to seek clinical or self-diagnosis. Forcing yourself to suffer without support will do nothing other than hold you back from your full leadership potential. Stop listening to people that talk about the overdiagnosis of ADHD and it being trendy. Whether you want a clinical or a self-diagnosis, learn everything you can about ADHD using reliable sources. Do lots of research so you are confident about the nuances of this condition and how it impacts you.

Now you know some of the ins and outs of ADHD diagnosis and the implications of being diagnosed. In the next chapter, I will show you just how important it is to find your fit.

5

Find Your Fit

Introduction

On your journey to success, you may have been convinced you have to lead just like everyone else (i.e., you have to be a neurotypical leader). But your brain is not wired like everyone else's. You differ in how you communicate, think, experience, and function, which can leave you feeling ostracized and incompetent. The more you try to fit in, the more you seem to stand out for the wrong reasons, because no matter how good you are at masking, the veneer will always crack at some point. Instead of an endless cycle of masking and cracking, we are going to take a different, less self-destructive approach. By learning about yourself and the tools and environment you need to succeed, you can begin to let go of fitting in and, instead, stand out for all the right reasons.

I would argue that our world is built to be most accommodating to those with neurotypical brains (I mean, neurodiverse people would never come up with a Monday to Friday, 9–5 work schedule. Am I right??). While there is nothing wrong with being neurotypical, there is also nothing wrong with being neurodiverse. So why would you force your brain to work in a way it isn't set up for? This is not to say that we should abandon all hope of working cohesively with neurotypical peers. They are not the enemy; their linear thinking can balance our associative/non-linear thinking. The point I am highlighting here is the ADHD tendency to repress and suffocate the elements of yourself that do not align with the neurotypical expectations in professional settings. It might feel like you *have* to mask, mold, suppress, repress, and suffocate. But I'm going to show you why the exact opposite is true. Why be "just ok" at trying to be someone else when you can be extraordinary at being yourself? When you spend all of your time at work masking, you have extinguished all of the best things that make you, you. What differentiates you as an excellent leader is now buried under layers of trying to "fake it 'til you make it".

I became a leader because I wanted to "do better" than the examples I had as a bedside nurse. I wanted to take care of our nursing staff to ensure they had a voice and the support they needed to have a happy and healthy professional life. Coming into one of my director roles, I was the sixth director in as many years. Needless to say, employee satisfaction scores were abysmal. However, I knew we had work to do, and I felt confident I had what it took to lead this team to get it done. So, I went in, rolled up my sleeves, and was my whole, unedited self with our staff. They saw the good, the bad, and the ugly. We had some rough patches, but overall, it worked wonders. During my tenure, our department converted our obstetric triage into an obstetric emergency department. We brought on an obstetric hospitalist group. We opened a robotic gynecologic operating room within our department that ran efficiently and effectively alongside our normal labor and delivery operations. We improved patient outcomes and provider relations, and skyrocketed employee engagement by 20 percent overall. Some survey subsets saw an over 40 percent increase in only a year. Not too shabby, right? Our accomplishments resulted from being able to be my real and best self with our team.

While I succeeded in being my unedited self with my team, I did not feel the same support to unmask with the executive leadership team and my director peers. I was too much, not enough, and not like them. But in making it unsafe for me to be, well, me, they missed out on seeing the best of what I had to offer and instead saw only the worst, leading to my resignation. You may be the sweetest, juiciest peach in the world, but you can always find someone who hates peaches. C'est la vie. The good news is, there are *tons* of peach appreciators out there, so let's go out and find them.

As we elaborate on why it is critical to find *your* fit, we're going to cover the fact that the odds are pretty good that you will never not have ADHD. We're also going to talk about how "mean girls" are everywhere, but we're going to ask ourselves, "Why do you want a spot at their table, and why do we fight so hard to surround ourselves with people that suck??" Next, I'm going to take you from feeling unfit to finding your fit, because this is YOUR life and YOUR leadership journey, and no one gets to say you are doing it wrong when you are doing your best. The final element of this chapter is our dive into ADHDers as entrepreneurs and why we can be so good at being our own boss.

Like forever-ever??

It is probable that you will always have ADHD. It was a long-held belief that people grew out of ADHD, and that it was only a childhood affliction, but the evidence tells us that that is not the case for most people. Dr. Margaret H. Sibley (psychologist, researcher, professor, and author specializing in ADHD) et al., published an article titled "Variable Patterns of Remission From ADHD in the Multimodal Treatment Study of ADHD" in the February 2022 issue of *The American Journal of Psychiatry*. Their research suggests that over 90 percent of children with ADHD will continue to experience residual symptoms beyond childhood. The results noted that some patients report periods of "remission" from their ADHD symptoms in adulthood. Still, the evidence shows that patients reported periods of both symptom remission and recurrence across the lifespan. Admittedly, there is a wide variation of data from study to study. Still, based on the research findings, a little over 9 percent of patients will reach a point where ADHD symptoms no longer impact them. I want to be clear; I'm not talking about a cure. At the time of writing this book, there was no cure for ADHD. I'm talking about symptoms that have diminished or have been managed to the point where they no longer impact the individual's life. At first, it might feel like you want to be in that 9 percent, but by the end of this book, you will have the tools you need to succeed, whether you end up in the 9 percent or the

90 percent. If you hide from or deny your ADHD symptoms in the hopes that they will go away, you are wasting valuable time and energy better spent on finding ways to make ADHD work for you.

You might be a little disheartened reading this or think, "If I'm in the 9 percent, wouldn't it be a waste of time trying to optimize these symptoms if they're just going to go away?" My counter-argument is that the tools and support systems you put into place to manage your ADHD symptoms are fluid and flexible. You can add, remove, change or leave behind tools at any time when they no longer serve you. The goal is to perform at your best in every phase of your life, whatever that looks like for you.

Is it overwhelming to think that you may be among the 90 percent that are managing these symptoms for the rest of your life? Allow me to reframe this thought process. When you look at ADHD as only a burden with no benefit, of course it is nerve wracking, and like you are carrying that weight forever (remember our Greek friend Sisyphus from Chapter One, rolling the rock up the mountain?). But what does it feel like to know that you will be more creative, intuitive, empathetic, hyperfocused, and many other wonderful things for the rest of your life? I don't hate that thought. Do you?

You might find it hard to reverse a negative view of your ADHD that has been reinforced your whole life. Take an index card and list all the ways that your bullet-train brain has served you well as a leader. Keep it on your nightstand, in your wallet, or somewhere close by where you can reference it when you are worried about the lifelong partnership with ADHD.

On Wednesdays, we wear pink

Mean girls are everywhere, and for some reason, society has turned that into the "cool" way to be. It's hard to avoid the pull of the popular kids. Who knew we'd be dealing with these cliques long after leaving high school? But take a step back and ask yourself why you want a spot at their table anyway?

Everyone knows a mean girl—maybe many of them—and to be honest, they're not just girls. Men can be mean too. They're petty, catty, fickle, fake, and two-faced. Barf. I want to make an important distinction here; in saying "mean girls", I'm not talking about people that disagree with you or those you might not invite to happy hour. You might not like hearing it, but you do need respectful dissenters in your life, and you don't have to be best friends with someone for them to help you grow. Mean girls are the people that make active attempts to tear you down. Unfortunately, they may have gained their success by stepping on the backs of others. You may envy their position, prestige, and popularity at work, and it may feel like something is wrong with you because you are never invited to join their table. I urge you to consider this, "Do you want to be planted or buried?". That's the difference in surrounding yourself with people that help you grow versus those that want to see you six feet under (in a professional sense, hopefully not a literal one!).

We are unearthing the real and ideal you so that nothing stands in your way of reaching your potential as a leader. You will not positively impact your life or the lives of your team if you surround yourself with negativity and self-doubt. By chasing the acceptance of people who don't deserve what you have to offer in the first place, you diminish the exceptional value you bring to the table.

I once had a boss (the use of the word boss instead of leader is intentional here) who ruled with an iron fist. Her office was separated from the main hallway by two large wooden doors and the administrative common area. Still, when she yelled at you, anyone walking in that hallway could hear it with a level of clarity equal to that of being in the room. At the time, I was one of three nurse managers that reported to her. We were all young, ambitious, hardworking, and intelligent. We had dreams of executive leadership, and because we had a lot in common, the three of us formed a strong bond from the beginning. We leaned on one another as we learned to be leaders, and together, we worked our way through the challenges and successes. It seemed ideal, but it did not last long. Our boss created and fostered a dog-eat-dog culture, sprinkling favoritism tempered with harsh criticism in such an inconsistent manner that made tensions rise. Eventually, it was made clear that there was only room for one of us to be promoted, and who it might be was anyone's guess depending on the day.

One of the managers (a wonderful human I attended college with) ended up leaving for her mental health. She had a young family and did not have any desire to tolerate the toxicity any longer. She had the courage and strength to take a stand even though it was difficult. She knew exactly how to protect her energy and never let anyone turn her into someone she didn't recognize in the mirror. We keep in touch from time to time, and she is still just as lovely, with a beautiful family and an unbreakable spirit.

The second manager and I were best friends and almost inseparable. We were each other's strength during the worst times and support during the best times. But, as one might predict, our friendship did not stop our boss from trying to turn us against one another, and sometimes it worked. I lashed out at this woman more times than a best friend ever should. It was awful. We were both ambitious with lofty career goals, chasing the unattainable favor of a woman happy to sit back and watch us go at each other's throats.

I was the next one to leave. After a year and a half, I packed my truck and my dog and moved 1,700 miles away in an attempt to heal and escape the trauma of that experience. Due to unfortunate circumstances, my best friend and I lost touch. However, I could not be prouder to share that she is now the director of nursing over that entire campus. Everything she has achieved is because instead of being broken down by what we experienced, she learned how not to be. Now that it's her turn to run the show, she leads by example, not by fear.

The moral of the story is, don't fight for a seat at the table of people who suck.

Now, what if the influential people above you are mean girls? Does that mean that you have to play the game to get ahead? In my experience, you cannot win against mean girls, and the risks of playing their game outweigh the benefits. Your unique skills and talents as a leader with ADHD earn you a spot at the *right* tables. You need to get out there and find them or, better yet, build them yourself. Greatness does not come from playing their game. It comes from mastering yours.

To circle back on what I mentioned at the beginning of the chapter, mean girls are not people that just disagree with you or ones that you are not friends with. I want you to ask yourself,

"Is this person bringing up valid counterarguments I can learn from?"

"Is this person someone that just rubs me the wrong way but isn't sabotaging me or trying to hinder my growth?"

Knowing the answers to these questions will help you differentiate between the people teaching you hard lessons and those that are trying to bury you.

I want you to think about how many mean girls you're chasing right now. How would it feel to let go of the notion that you have to play their game to get ahead? Write a list of your unique skills and talents. If you're not sure, ask your friends and supporters. Now write a list of the people you work best with, those who bring out the best in you as a leader. Look at the commonalities and consider what you can learn from these people. Even if you don't get along as friends, you still have a great growth opportunity with them.

If your leader is a mean girl, you might feel like you have no choice in the matter. Remember, there is always a choice. You are not a tree. If your environment does not serve you, pick yourself up and move on.

Mold breaker

Now it's time to talk about going from being unfit to finding your fit. Are you made to feel as though you are "less than", "not enough", "too much", or "all the wrong stuff", i.e., unfit? That is because you are not the clay that goes into the mold but a hand-sculpted masterpiece. You need to find and/or create your fit. Now, I am not talking about finding a "perfect" situation. There is no such thing. But, just like when I spoke about romance, there is such a thing as perfect for *you*. After so many years of hearing all the ways that you're just not "it", it may feel like there is some truth to the idea that the problem is you. In reality, your strength as a leader comes from breaking the mold instead of trying to fit into it.

Important to note here that you can never hope to reach your full potential in the wrong environment. If you took the most stunning tropical plant and placed it in the desert, it would have no chance of thriving. The same goes for you, you beautiful hibiscus. (I'm the epitome of a gray thumb. Gardeners, don't come after me if hibiscus plants can, in fact, survive in the desert. You know what I was trying to say.)

After resigning from my first director role and searching for something new, I landed in a clinical value analysis director role (fancy words to say that I used my clinical expertise to help hospitals decide which products helped achieve the best patient outcomes while maintaining cost-effectiveness). Did I love the work? Nope. But when I say I had the best leader in this role, y'all . . . I had the BEST leader. Her name is Bonnie Solitaire (called you out, boss lady!!). She is compassionate, insightful, supportive, intelligent, firm but fair, development-oriented, and the greatest advocate an employee could ever ask for. This small snippet doesn't do her even an ounce of justice, but no words ever could. I raved about this woman to the extent that when my sister started a new role under a leader she loved, she called me and said, "Gwen, I found *my* Bonnie!"

Under Bonnie's guidance, I flourished. I stayed in that role longer than any role I'd held before it. Not because I loved the job, but because I was working for someone who, in every sense of the concept, helped make me better. I went through my second master's program in that role and can say without hesitation that I am a better person and leader because I was led and uplifted by this woman. I went from being asked to resign from a toxic environment to being recommended for corporate office roles in the very next position. This was because someone believed in me and not only saw my value but nourished it and promoted it to others. I am living proof that your environment is everything. If you are feeling unfit, get out there and find your fit.

You might read this and think, "Not everyone has the luxury to change jobs whenever they want." This is true. There are many reasons why you might be stuck in a role or an environment that is not the best fit for you—whether financial, geographical, relational, etc.—and I respect every single one of them. I urge you to find your fit because you cannot reach the full extent of your potential in the wrong environment. If you're stuck for now, find the space that works for you whenever you are able.

In the table below, write the top five things that come to mind when you consider what makes you feel fit versus what makes you feel unfit.

What makes me feel fit?	What makes me feel unfit?
E.g. Being asked for my opinion in strategy planning	My opinion on strategy is ignored or dismissed

After reviewing the table above, how many items from the fit column does your current role or environment check off? How about how many from the unfit column? Consider this, if you are feeling or being made to feel unfit, what is stopping you from seeking a better fit?

As I mentioned above, it might be impossible to leave your current role for a variety of reasons. Weigh the pros and cons. Make a list of why you need to stay in this place and compare it to a list of ways that being in this place is hindering or harming you. Is there a compromise that can be made or a timeline that can be established for when a change would be more feasible if it is not right now?

Pros of leaving	Cons of leaving
E.g. I find a better fit	I might have to take a pay cut

You don't have to make these decisions right away. These exercises are all about building awareness. It might mean you need to make a plan and be patient, but that's the idea; to start the ball rolling.

Being your own boss

ADHDers are in a unique and prime position to be successful as entrepreneurs. Why are we so good at being our own boss? It's not because we are lousy team players or want to be in charge of everyone. It's because our creativity, associative thinking, and innovative talents set an excellent foundation for being an entrepreneur. When I say entrepreneur, I am not only talking about the Sir Richard Bransons of the world. I am talking about anyone who takes on the task of starting their own company, business, service, etc. It might feel like you could never be an entrepreneur, but ADHD brains have optimal wiring to make this a fruitful career path for some of us. I'll go into more detail about this in a moment.

The right fit for you may never be in working for someone else. If this describes your situation, knowing how your neurodiversity can support you in entrepreneurship can give you the confidence to say, "Why not me?"

Some of the world's most successful entrepreneurs have your type of beautiful and different brain wiring—Sir Richard Branson, founder of Virgin; David Neeleman, founder of JetBlue Airways; Diane Swonk, economist and author; and Charles Schwab, founder and chairman of Charles Schwab and Co., to name a few.

In my interview with Brooke Schnittman (first mentioned in Chapter Three), she revealed that the current evidence suggests that

35 percent of entrepreneurs have ADHD. I believe this number is higher in actuality if you factor in those that remain undiagnosed and unaware that they have it, but that's where the statistics stand right now. Brooke believes that passion, drive and the ability to overcome failures are three things that make some ADHDers choose the entrepreneurial path. She says, "Nothing can stop an ADHDer from just hyper-focusing on the things that really drive them, and usually what makes that change is when there is an experience that they want to move past." The experience could be something like not getting along with a boss or not wanting to stay in a particular job and instead wanting to seek fulfillment and chase their passion.

Schnittman credits the success of many ADHD entrepreneurs to our ability to be determined, creative, and multifaceted in our skillset. You can "learn as you go" instead of being trapped in "needing to know everything before you get started" with a venture of interest. As I mentioned, you might have to build your own table to sit at. ADHD can give you the perfect edge to do just that.

If you think, "I'm not like those people. I can't just quit my job and dive headfirst into starting a company." No one said that you had to or should quit your job and dive headfirst into anything. We are an impulsive bunch, so that may be where your head goes because we often tend to have an all-or-nothing mentality. For most people, the smartest way to do it is to try your business model as a side hustle while maintaining full- or part-time employment. This allows you to test things out and see if you could scale up as it grows until it becomes your primary source of income.

For example, I started a home bakery business. I have enjoyed baking as a hobby for a long time. Over time, I began to receive so many requests for baked goods during the holidays it became challenging to keep everyone's orders straight. In an impulsive moment, I decided to make it an official side business. The resulting hyperfixation from the excitement allowed me to get an entire website with an ordering system up and running in less than two days. I never intended that business to be my primary income because I didn't want to be a full-time baker—and that's okay too. I shut down the website a year later and resolved to be better at setting boundaries around which baking requests I could fill and which I could not. My second foray into the land of entrepreneurs was the END (Excellence in Neurodiversity) Institute. I created this collaborative to be a safe space for neurodiverse professionals and leaders to share stories and best practices, find resources, connect with like-minded, ambitious individuals, and a source of advocacy and education supporting ADHD and neurodiversity in the workplace (I encourage you to join our community!). I took on both of these ventures while having a full-time and another part-time job.

However you approach entrepreneurship, it is all about growing through your journey and ensuring it fits your needs. For example, you may decide you don't want to work for yourself full-time, but starting a permanent side hustle is a good gig for you. You can make being an entrepreneur work for your life in many different ways. Explore the options.

Do you have an idea for a business or company you've been keeping in the back of your mind, and it just won't go away?

Draw up a one-page business proposal. What are you selling? Who will buy it, and why do they need it? If this seems too big a task, start by listing all the best business ideas you have ever had. Then pick three and test them out on friends. Which, if any, gets the most support? Keep working through your list until you find something you love, and others love too.

You may be thinking, "Gwen, it is not feasible for me to start my own company. How many times do I have to say this?" Of course, entrepreneurship is not for everyone. I am not suggesting that every leader with ADHD run out and create a startup. But don't rule it out as an option because of your self-doubt, fear of the unknown, or concern that you are just not good enough. Remember, if you want to work for yourself, why not?

📋 IN SUMMARY

In this chapter, you have learned that 90 percent of you will have ADHD for the rest of your life, but surrounding yourself with the right people and environments will set you up to make ADHD work wonders for you. It can be challenging to resist the urge to fit in, but by choosing to find *your* fit, you will also find your voice, fulfillment, and best self in leadership. This may mean you strike out on your own and try your hand at entrepreneurship. You are wired to be a leader, but that can mean many things, and it does not have to be limited to just leading within someone else's infrastructure. Stop chasing the approval of shitty people and trying to force yourself to fit in places where you will not thrive. Instead, start getting comfortable with finding your fit and evaluating your potential as an entrepreneur.

Now that we've talked about how powerful it is to find the right fit for you, I want to dive into a topic that impacts most ADHDers deeply: how much shame there is in "should".

6

The Shame in "Should"

Introduction

Your entire life, you have been told what you should and should not do. These "shoulds" are based on the opinions of people who have played formative roles for you during your leadership journey and across your life—a reflection of their individual views of morality, measures of success, and societal norms. The problem with "shoulds" is that they never take everyone into account. What a leader *should* be, looks different in different industries, within different teams, across different generations, and even in different geographical locations.

Picture this, your ADHD brain is a giant diamond and every "should" is a piece of fine mesh covering it like a shroud. You may still see the sparkles from the gem under the first few layers, but before long, all you see is a dark ball of mesh with no hint of the beautiful brilliance beneath. By allowing yourself to be engulfed in shrouds of "should", you lose every ounce of sparkle that made you a great leader and a great person in the first place.

Sing it with me, "This little light of mine; I'm gonna let it shine, let it shine, let it shine, let it shine."

"Should" is what society and the people in your life expect of you. These are guardrails put into place by your friends, family, loved ones, coworkers, faith, etc. The code you are meant to conduct yourself by, which no self-respecting person would want to deviate from if you ask them. Lucky for you, in just a few pages, we will talk about why you don't want to ask them and who you should ask instead.

Disclaimer: When I say I want you to challenge neurotypical society's "should" and instead find your own version, I am not advocating for you to go rogue and start breaking laws. Please don't push someone off a cliff when they annoy you (we've all thought about it). Or drive 110 miles an hour down the highway because it feels good. Some "shoulds" are put into place to help keep you and other humans generally safe. I am advocating that you re-evaluate which "shoulds" tell you to keep quiet because others find you too loud. Which ones tell you to shrink yourself because others say you're too much. And which ones say to hide everything you are because others feel you don't fit. At this point in your life, it may feel like you need to embrace the societal "should" if you want to get ahead, but if you read the introduction, you know you were not made to fit in. You were made to stand out. And stand out you shall.

When you allow your unique leadership strengths to be stifled by expectations designed with neurotypical people in mind, you struggle to reach your full potential or even stay afloat. Aligning your "shoulds" with the way your ADHD brain works will take your capabilities as a leader to new heights. According to the well-known quote, "If you judge a fish by its ability to climb a tree, it will spend its entire life thinking that it is stupid." Should is, by nature, relative and a huge source of shame for those with ADHD. There is no shortage of these expectations in the world, but when was the last time we asked 'should' according to whom?

In this chapter, we will challenge the assertion that those with ADHD lack self-awareness, discuss how and when to take feedback, talk about why we must never be afraid to try, try again, and review why coaching can change the game.

The self-awareness stigma

Those with ADHD have a reputation for lacking self-awareness. I disagree with that assertion and have found the complete opposite to be true in many cases. Neurodiverse individuals with ADHD are often hyper-aware of themselves and how they present to the world because we have been told our entire lives that everything about us is wrong. Suppose we didn't know how the world saw us and how significant the gap is between how we are perceived and what is expected of us in many instances. Why would we spend so much energy masking and trying to behave like we are neurotypical?

Self-awareness is the ability to view yourself as the outside world views you. It is my belief that people claim ADHDers are not self-aware because we are still held to the standards of being neurotypical. How we communicate and behave may seem like we are unaware of how others perceive us in professional and social settings. Still, the reality is that we do not understand or relate to many of the ways that the neurotypical world operates. Our communication and behavior make sense to us. The fact that it may not make sense to others does not mean we aren't aware of our actions. It means we do not act as a neurotypical person might in the same situation

I am not claiming that there is no such thing as someone with ADHD who is not self-aware. However, we must stop equating self-awareness with behaving and communicating within the boundaries of the neurotypical standard. It may feel like you need to hide the real you to achieve self-awareness, but that could not be further from the truth. Self-awareness is the foundation for personal and professional growth. Mastering this skill without masking or being hyper-critical of yourself will allow you to pinpoint your areas for improvement while identifying strengths you may not have known you possessed.

It was baffling to me when I read multiple ADHD books and articles stating that individuals with ADHD are lacking in self-awareness. I am not exaggerating when I say I spend almost every waking moment thinking about what I am doing and how others are responding to it.

"Did Karen just poke Cheryl in the ribs because they think what I'm saying is stupid?"

"Oh, no, Lacey just furrowed her brow when I laughed. I was too loud."

"Ryan just stopped talking when I walked around the corner. Does that mean they were talking about me?"

During one of the many times I sat in the HR office throughout that infamous first director role, I was being written up for a complaint raised by an employee about my communication. The HR partner was describing the complaint, and I was sharing details of the conversation in question from my perspective. At one point I said, "I am extremely self-aware," and, without hesitating, the HR person said, "You're not as self-aware as you think you are."

Ouch.

Also, inaccurate.

This was an example of the self-awareness stigma that surrounds ADHD. I did not (and do not) interact with the world in a neurotypical fashion for the simple reason that I am not neurotypical. That does not mean I do not know how I behave or communicate. It means that how I behave and communicate may not make sense to you. You cannot understand why, so you believe I must not know because no one would obviously choose to act this way, right? We are fish being judged by our inability to climb a tree instead of being celebrated for our ability to swim.

The notion that having ADHD means that you are not self-aware is not just inaccurate but damaging. Self-awareness is a foundational skill for every leader. It is important not to confuse being self-aware with being neurotypical.

Now, you may think, "But I am unaware of myself at times. Gwen, even you wrote earlier about talking over other people in conversation and not realizing it, so it must be a real problem." I would argue that everyone, neurotypical or neurodiverse, has moments where they are not self-aware. My nephew, bless his little heart, chews with his mouth WIDE open when he's distracted—not because he is trying to be rude or gross, but because his mind is elsewhere. Intermittent moments like this are not the same as being unaware of oneself on a large scale. Having ADHD often means being accused of lacking self-awareness when, in reality, we almost always know what we're doing, and we do it because it makes sense to how our brain is wired.

Have you been accused of not being self-aware, but you feel like all you do is evaluate yourself and your interactions with the world? Below are three examples of how you can break these situations down. Start with the situation (what others saw), add your reality (how you saw it), and think about what you can do to avoid misunderstandings in the future.

Situation (what they saw)	Your reality (what you saw)	What to do
You were accused of being negative when asking a question in a strategy meeting.	You asked about a barrier you believe has the potential to derail the project and were trying to make sure it was addressed.	Explain your reality so there is no room for misinterpretation of your intentions. Then, ask for suggestions on bringing up similar issues in the future more positively. Consider whether this works for you.

Situation (what they saw)	Your reality (what you saw)	What to do
You were accused of being a bully when you called an employee out for being late to their shift in front of other employees.	You stated expectations that all employees be on time as per company policy and professional courtesy.	Have the conversation in private next time. Ensure you're setting the same expectations with all of your employees. Keep HR in the loop and document all concerns with performance or behavior, so you can demonstrate patterns and how you're addressing the concerns.
You were accused of being unprofessional for laughing too much at a joke that a candidate made during an interview.	You did laugh at the joke because it was funny, and you like to bring humanity and authenticity to your role as a leader. You are not embarrassed to laugh.	Have a candid conversation with the executive team about their expectations and definition of professional behavior. If you're uncomfortable with how the conversation goes, consider how many of the expectations are out of alignment with the type of leader you want to be.

Does the concept of neurotypical behavior being confused with self-awareness resonate with you and your experiences? Being neurodiverse does not give you a pass from self-awareness. It is still essential as a leader. The key is understanding that self-awareness is not equivalent to forcing yourself to behave as if you are neurotypical. As I once did, you might feel that self-awareness is a curse. What good is knowing you're doing things deemed unprofessional if your brain cannot operate in any other way? Let me offer you comfort. Your brain does not need to operate any other way than it does right now. You possess everything necessary to be an exceptional leader between your ears already. When a flower does not bloom, you change the environment, not the flower. Just some plant food for thought (not sorry for the corny joke).

Be salty

ADHDers NEED feedback. We overthink and ruminate, so knowing where we are doing well and where we can improve is important. That being said, it is even more important to be discerning about the feedback that you allow in—the "shoulds" of how to live, lead, or run your business. I am here to tell you not to be afraid of filtering most of it out. I am not saying to ignore or disregard *every* piece of advice you receive. On the contrary, the right kind of feedback from the right kind of people can be essential to building self-awareness and continual development. You might be wondering how to figure out which feedback to allow in and which to filter out. Throughout this section, you will find specific strategies that make feedback filtering simple and effective.

Focusing on the wrong feedback is like drinking out of a firehose. Too much coming at you all at once will tear your face off. Ok, that was dramatic, but seeking out and internalizing too much of the wrong feedback will hinder your growth, stifle your strengths and point you in a direction you never intended to go. Knowing the who, what and why of filtering feedback is the fastest way to drown out the unnecessary and often harmful background noise.

Mark Zheng is the president of a Los Angeles-based sizeless clothing company, Sene. Sene is a custom clothing brand that, according to the video on their 'About' webpage, was born from the knowledge that standard clothing sizes are not the answer for the significant diversity of body types that we all exist in. They believe there is far too much environmentally harmful waste within the standard-size clothing industry (US$5 billion of waste is produced each year within this industry), and customers deserve an individualized approach to the clothing they wear every day (Zheng 2021).

The CEO of the startup, Ray Li, has this simple but profound advice that keeps his eye on the prize at Sene, "Take feedback from customers seriously. Take feedback from everyone else with a mountain of salt" (Li 2022). Not just a grain, guys. A mountain! Let that sink in for a minute. Even if you are not (yet) a CEO or do not have customers in the traditional sense, which people in your life do you serve? Who do you live for? Who do you go to work for? These are your customers. If you would not go to someone for solid, reliable advice, they belong on the top of your mountain of salt, not in your ear.

I do not know Li personally, and as far as I'm aware, he does not have ADHD. However, I include this story because his message is so important and has direct applicability to how ADHDers can optimize feedback. Of course, not all feedback is created equal. You must make wise choices when determining which feedback you allow to influence your behavior and which does not align with your goals.

You may be in a situation where you think you have no choice but to take feedback from someone who should be in the salt pile. Maybe you report to them, or they somehow influence your career potential. Remember, you are building your leadership skills. If your supervisor or someone in a position of influence over your career is not someone you respect or trust enough to go to for advice, is there anything that can be done to rectify that? Can you have a conversation with them to help create a more helpful and constructive feedback system that will further your progress toward your goals? If you can't have a conversation like that, are you sure you want that type of person to have so much influence over your future?

Be careful not to discount someone's feedback just because you dislike what they have to say. Sometimes the most difficult feedback can be the most important. We may shy away from it or block it out because we do not like the mouthpiece it comes out of, but these can often be the most formative types of feedback.

If you are unsure if this person is an appropriate source of feedback, ask yourself these questions:

- Is this someone I respect and trust enough for their advice, even if I don't like them on a personal level?

- Are they giving me constructive and actionable feedback versus being degrading or cruel without guidance on improving?
- Does this person represent the voice of my customer?—in a traditional sense, if you are an entrepreneur, or in an overall sense, meaning the voice of the people you serve as a leader.

ADHDers tend to be hyper-critical, and when you are in a leadership position, you feel like your every move is under a microscope. You must take feedback from all angles, right? Not if you want to reach your full potential. You're giving humanity way too much credit by believing that everyone gives worthwhile feedback. Quality over quantity.

How much feedback have you allowed that only serves to wound you instead of helping you reach your goals? Use the following questions to guide you as you work on filtering feedback.

- Does the feedback include actionable items?
  - e.g., Are you given suggestions on what to do to improve?
- Does the feedback center around an ADHD symptom?
  - e.g., Being told it is rude to take notes during a conversation, but you use that as a tool to help your working memory.
- Does the feedback center on facts and not emotions?
  - e.g., "You were three days late in delivering the employee engagement action plan, delaying our presentation to the board." Versus, "I feel like you laugh too loud when you're checking in on your staff members in the morning."

- Does the person delivering the feedback and/or the environment in which you work provide support for the identified areas of improvement?
  - e.g., If you can never get the schedule out on time, is it appropriate to delegate that task to a member of your team that will be able to complete it on time?
- Are you discerning in whom you accept feedback from and whom you place on the summit of salt mountain as Li tells us to do?
- Whom would you go to for advice, and who do you respect because of their leadership qualities and skills? Are you getting feedback from them?
- Consider who your customer is in the traditional sense— you want them to purchase your goods or services, or in the metaphorical sense—you serve them as their leader and are responsible for their development. What feedback can those customers offer?

ADHD tends to make you focus on the negative, so it may be hard to let go of feedback when you receive it, even if it is not valuable or constructive. Remember, if you wouldn't go to that person for advice, don't make them your primary source of feedback.

If, at first, you don't succeed . . .

When you are working to find your version of "should", don't be afraid to try again. You have lived under the shame of other people's "shoulds" your whole life; it is not easy to shake off and view yourself in a new light. You won't get it right the first time and will fall back into old habits occasionally, but keep trying.

Living and leading with authenticity is what will make you exceptional. Your version of should is the life and leadership style that works for you. It means moving the guardrails to frame *your* road, not someone else's. When I say "live and lead with authenticity", I am not giving you license to use the excuse, "This is just how I am. Take it or leave it." Hard no to all of that. Authenticity does not permit you to be an unrepentant a$$hole. Be authentic to the strengths and diversity of thought that your brain wiring brings to the table. It may feel overwhelming to know you will stumble and fall as you rewrite what it looks like for you as a leader. You pride yourself on your work ethic and don't like to fail, but don't worry. You are never going to be a failure until you stop trying.

Through trial and error, you will learn where to place your guardrails to optimize your performance on your leadership journey. If you do not put in the effort of trying, making a mistake and then trying again, you will continue to live and lead under the constraints and weight of someone else's "shoulds". When you have a late diagnosis or undiagnosed ADHD, it is common to feel like you are going it alone. You struggle to find answers for why the neurotypical leadership roadmap does not work for you, and it is hard to know what you need on your path to success. Diagnosis can provide a sense of clarity, but it is not an all-encompassing how-to guide in learning about yourself and your brain. You will need to put in the work to determine what works for you. When you discover something that doesn't work, don't try to force it just because it may have worked for someone else. Let it go and move on.

For example, I am one of those people that can never keep up with journaling, despite knowing how helpful it can be to process thoughts and feelings. I always gave it my best efforts but never fell into a routine. For a while, I developed the habit of buying new journals every time I went to the store to try to entice myself to keep up the practice. "This gorgeous old-fashioned leather one is certain to pull me out of this writing rut!!" Maybe not. When the inevitable happened, and I let it fall by the wayside for the 5,000th time, I used to shame myself, but what good did that do? I am not motivated by shame; it only makes me feel worse. These days, I'm comfortable admitting that I'm not good at journaling and I stopped buying new ones. Does journaling work for some people with ADHD? Without a doubt. For me, nope. But that's ok.

ADHD has a different presentation for everyone, which means your secret formula for success will be different than anyone else's. Keep trying, and don't be ashamed of what does and doesn't work for you. Your superhero cape is going to be a patchwork quilt, and there's nothing wrong with that. Your "should" must be your own if you want to remove the shroud of shame and find the power-house leader in yourself.

Maybe you don't know how to figure out which "shoulds" are your own and which were imposed by external sources. The deeper they are ingrained, the harder it is to figure this out. That is ok, and it will take time to figure out what your most authentic self wants and needs. Evaluate your habits, your patterns and your behavior at work. What would you do differently if no one was there to tell you that it was wrong or out of place? Do any habits spring to mind when we talk about shaking off shame and redefining your "should"? In my time as a leader, a should that I threw in the trash is that leaders should not have strong personal and emotional connections with their teams. My entire career has been in healthcare. The bond formed among nurses is remarkable. We see it all when caring for patients at the bedside, and we are able to get through it all because we do it together—the best of the best and the worst of the worst.

As a nursing leader, that ability to connect with my team on a deeper level where I knew them as people, not just nurses—and they knew me the same way—was paramount to our success. I laughed with them, cried with them and felt frustrated with them. I supported them just as they supported me. I loved them for every bit of who they were. To this day, some of those nurses tell me I am the best leader they have had in all of their years (sometimes decades) on the job. My empathy is one of my greatest strengths, and by trashing the idea that I should separate myself on an emotional level from my team, I was able to build a rapport with them that was second to none.

How does it make you feel thinking about the trial and error of different ADHD-specific methods to support you, the life you want to live and the leader you want to be? Is it scary? Don't be afraid. You will not be trying and failing; you will be trying and growing. If your current place of employment is one where you are expected to conform and lead within the confines of a neurotypical standard, you might be anxious. You may worry that you will not be supported in trying different tactics to find your sweet spot. Start by having a conversation with your team or your leader if you are not currently at the top of the internal hierarchy. Share that you want to perform at your best and would like to play around with different approaches or tools to help you be the best leader you can, and come prepared with specifics.

For example, if you are talking to your leader, you could say, "I would like to pilot a more informal approach to employee check-ins. The templated format feels inauthentic to me, and I believe I can create a stronger rapport with my staff if I am allowed more freedom to go off script and allow the conversation to flow more naturally. What are your thoughts on that?"

If they turn you down, see if they would be willing to try something else that might meet your needs or at least explain why they cannot support your request. In the end, it is up to you to decide where you are comfortable working and leading. Only you can make the call as to whether an environment that does not support your best work is a good fit for your professional aspirations.

Put me in coach

It can be hard to shake off years (or decades) of shame from all the ways you're not what you "should" be. Sometimes we might need a little help, and there is certainly no shame in that. Enlisting the help of a coach who specializes in ADHD can be a game changer in helping us identify and eliminate thoughts and habits stopping us from achieving our goals.

The word "coach" gets thrown around quite a lot these days because anyone can call themselves a coach. What I mean by "coach" is someone who specializes in ADHD, has lived experience or at least education that makes them a credible source of information and guidance, and may even have credentials or certifications in ADHD coaching. I am not talking about the "overnight experts" trying to make a quick buck by attracting as many clients as possible without providing meaningful help.

Having ADHD means that we can struggle with framing our ideas and plans with clarity or the execution of those plans once we have clarity. If we do not have the right support, we can stagnate in our career growth, our businesses might fail before they have a chance to get started, and we may never reach our full potential. On one of our morning commute calls, Brooke Schnittman shared that she has had clients who tripled their revenue after just one month of working with her. Of course, that is not a guarantee, just an example of how impactful having the right coach can be.

Brooke shared the basics of her program with me to give you an idea of what a well-established program can look like. She and her team focus on students, leaders, and entrepreneurs, taking them through her patented "3C Activation" program, certified through the ICF. She works with her clients for 12 weeks to go from "chaos to clarity" in group and individual settings based on their needs. The first four weeks focus on getting to the root of what is going on in the client's life. She calls it "clearing the chaos". The next four weeks focus on "1 percent improvements" at a time, implementing tools to help with scheduling, organization, planning, etc. Here the clients begin to use a habit-stacking method to build the framework for positive change. The last four weeks are where the stretch goals come in. This means working on uncomfortable conversations, delegating, and taking on bigger challenges. The increased confidence the clients have gained in the first eight weeks of the program sets them up to be ready to face these challenges head-on. Over the past four years, Brooke has grown her coaching business from just herself to an entire team of coaches and support staff. Despite being one herself, she acknowledged that she also hired coaches to help her tackle new situations or experiences with which she did not have previous experience.

You may think, "I can't afford a coach. It's just not a financial priority for me right now." That is a valid concern. Coaching can seem like quite an investment, but that's just what it is, an investment. If you've been spinning your wheels, not getting ahead, or are unhappy but have no idea what comes next, a good coach can help you move the needle. Say you land a promotion as a result of working with a coach. What type of a raise would you receive? Compare that to the cost of coaching. Or maybe you're a business owner that can increase their revenue two or threefold by working with a coach. The return on investment can be well worth it if you work with the right people.

When you hire a coach, how do you know who to trust when it seems like "coaches" are everywhere? I asked Brooke for her advice in finding a quality ADHD coach, and this is what she had to say:

- Seek word-of-mouth recommendations from friends or trusted connections who have experience with a coach.

How did they like the program? Did they find value in what the coach offered? What was the outcome for them after participating in the program?

- Use reputable sources like ADD.org and CHADD.org to find vetted experts in your area. Beware of the overnight experts.

- Schedule a "discovery call" with the coach (this should be free of charge). Use that time to evaluate your fit. Are you a good match? Do you like their approach and their program structure?

- Look at their background.
  - Do they have experience with the problems you are trying to solve or the goals you are setting for yourself? If not, do you feel they could effectively guide you in these areas?
  - Do they have credentials or certifications from organizations like ADHD Coach Academy (ADDCA) or JST Coaching & Training? Are they ICF certified?
    - Certifications are not everything and do not guarantee a great coach. This is just a point to consider.

Remember, you can change coaches along the way. A coach you sign on with today may not meet your needs in six months, and there is nothing wrong with that. Make sure any agreement you sign with a coach allows you to move on if it is not a good fit or you no longer need their level of expertise.

📋 IN SUMMARY

In this chapter, you have learned that the shame in "should" can crush you if you let it. By reclaiming the right to define your own version of what your life and leadership journey should look like, you are clearing the path to success. It has been said that we are an unaware bunch, but I am going to be firm in planting my flag against that assertion. We are often self-aware on an acute level—that doesn't mean that we are transformed by magic into being neurotypical.

Be discerning about who you take feedback from and let everyone else sit in the salt. Don't be afraid to try again (unless you're skydiving. In that case, please get it right the first time). You may have been skeptical about the benefits of a coach, but now you know how they can help you step up your game.

Stop shaming yourself for a lifetime of never being what other people say you should be. Instead, start redefining your leadership journey on your own terms. Then, align your actions to match that journey.

Now that you know how pivotal it is to step out from under the shroud of should, you can begin to pave your own path. In the next chapter, I will show how your body can be your ADHD brain's best friend.

7

Brain + Body = BFFs

Introduction

ADHD leaders often separate taking care of their body and their mind because, let's face it, it is a lot of work to take care of both when you are neurodiverse. Most of you know there is a direct correlation between physical health and mental health, so I won't belabor the point. But what you may not know is that ADHD comes with a unique set of challenges that can impact your ability to take optimal care of yourself. The benefits of physical health are not unique to ADHDers. Still, they are even more pronounced for you because a healthy body heightens our ability to capitalize on our mental strengths.

Despite the proven benefits, trying to achieve and maintain this healthy body can be difficult when ADHD symptoms present themselves in ways that seem to hinder much more than help (think impulsivity and dopamine-seeking habits). So, allow me to offer this sentiment of encouragement. Physical health does not have to be complicated. In short, it is just about fueling, moving and resting your body in ways that keep your brain—and the body that houses it—happy. You do not have to be an ultra-marathoner or exist on nothing but kale and grilled chicken breast to be healthy (I would dieeeeeee, but some people love living that way. Huge kudos to them because it takes a lot of dedication!). We're talking about whatever version of health works for *you* as a person and leader. In this chapter, we will reframe the way you think about health to remove anxiety and societal pressures. That's right, we're still shaking off those "shoulds" people!!

With the overwhelming amount of information available, it might feel like you will never figure out the "right" way to be healthy, but I will walk you through some simple tips to get you started. Obligatory disclaimer: while I'm a registered nurse, I am not a dietitian. I have a general knowledge of physical activity and nutrition, but I do not have formal training beyond what I received in nursing school, and I do not claim to be an expert on these matters. I am a leader with ADHD who has researched the following practices, applied them to my own life and recognized their benefits.

When your body is active, well rested, and receiving appropriate fuel, it sets your brain up for optimal functioning. Of course, this is true for neurotypical individuals as well, but for those with ADHD, it means better sleep, increased focus, less brain fog, better emotional regulation, and more happy brain chemicals. All are vital to performing at your best in your leadership role.

Your neurochemistry and your brain's ability to function are impacted directly by what you eat, how you move, and the quality and quantity of your sleep. We will dive into the research for each of these areas of health in the following sections. A healthy body is an excellent foundation for achieving optimal brain function with ADHD. As you may have guessed (at least I hope you have if you've been paying attention to these last couple of paragraphs), we are going to talk about three critical elements of taking care of your body when you have ADHD—nutrition, exercise and sleep. I will explain how ADHD impacts all of these areas in different ways and give you tips from experts to help you achieve and maintain long-term health.

Food for thought

A healthy approach to nutrition means fueling your brain and body with a good balance of the nutrients you need to perform at your best. Let's get something out of the way right off the bat. When I talk about a healthy approach, I am *not* talking about a specific diet or "good" versus "bad" food. That type of thinking will only hold you back. Throw it right out the window. I *am* talking about helping you build sustainable nutrition habits to support your best performance in life and as a leader. It may feel like you have tried everything under the sun and can't crack the code, but before this section is over, you will have four simple and actionable steps from an expert to get you started on your journey.

So why is nutrition so important for ADHDers? Evidence tells us that when your brain does not have the right fuel, your ADHD symptoms may worsen and create more significant hurdles for you to overcome on your path to success. Studies show that the macronutrient protein promotes alertness in the brain. In 1982, Dr. Richard J Wurtman, a medical doctor and neuroscience researcher at the Massachusetts Institute of Technology (MIT), published a study titled "Nutrients That Modify Brain Function" in the journal *Scientific American*. He found that protein triggers alertness, inducing neurotransmitters. Fast forward to 2022, in the article "Change Your Diet, Find Your Focus" published in *ADDitute* magazine, the editors write, "Proteins affect brain performance by providing the amino acids from which neurotransmitters are made. Neurotransmitters are biochemical messengers that carry signals from one brain cell to another. The better you feed these messengers, the more efficiently and accurately they can deliver the goods, allowing your child to be alert at school or you to be more on top of things at work."

Rebecca King MS, RDN, LDN is a registered dietitian and nutritionist diagnosed with ADHD at 19 years old. She discovered her passion in a dietitian program in college and has since woven her education and personal experience into her work. Rebecca is a successful nutrition coach for clients with ADHD. I sat down with her to talk about the nuances of eating habits for ADHDers. I felt validated by how much our conversation resonated with my personal experience and relationship with food.

Rebecca and I discussed how the usual advice given to neurotypical individuals—like spending a whole day every week meal prepping, restrictive elimination diets, or complex meal plans—does not work well for ADHDers. Despite this, so few resources are available tailored to our brain wiring. The research is very limited, and most professionals in the nutrition space (coaches, nutritionists, dietitians, etc.) do not understand why people with ADHD struggle to adhere to their plans. This can lead to clients being shamed when they can't do these "simple things" like non-ADHDers can.

Because she knows how overwhelming and unrealistic most of the traditional healthy eating advice can be for a neurodiverse brain, Rebecca shared with me four simple principles that provide a foundation for better nutrition with ADHD:

1. eating something every three to four hours
2. exploring other sources of stimulation besides food
3. prioritizing protein with every meal
4. removing the shame in whatever works for you.

These foundational principles are a great way to get started. No complex templates to stress over, no constant journals to forget about until the last minute, and no broad restrictions that can be hard to maintain. Four principles. You can totally do that!

Now that you have a foundation, I want to dive deeper into why balanced nutrition can be such a challenge for ADHDers in the first place. Let's start with the somewhat controversial one, ADHD medication. Some medications used in the treatment of ADHD can impact appetite. Appetite suppression can occur while the medication is active in your system, which may make it more difficult for you to recognize hunger cues throughout the day. If you don't feel hungry, you may not eat very much. When the evening rolls around and the effects of the medication wear off, you may feel ravenous because you haven't eaten in hours or possibly all day. You're so hungry that you binge eat as a result.

Do you find yourself eating when you are bored? No surprise there. The act of eating itself can be a source of stimulation for us when we're feeling understimulated. When we eat for stimulation, we often reach for carbohydrates (i.e., sugar) because they are a source of dopamine (which we know by now that ADHDers are always seeking due to lower baseline levels). Do not be ashamed if you're like me and use food this way. There is nothing wrong with eating for stimulation. Here are some tips to help maintain that healthy balance while doing so:

- Allow it to be stimulating. Rebecca talks about "savoring the moment" so you get the highest mental reward possible from what you are eating.
- Eliminate distractions as much as possible. Give 100 percent of your attention to the food and the act of eating it.
- Be mindful. Pay attention to how your body responds as you eat and after you are done. Do your best to stop when you are full.
- Repeat this practice whenever you eat for stimulation to help identify what hungry, full, understimulated, and satiated feel like.
- If you overeat, don't beat yourself up. Take a mental note of how overeating made your body feel and if it impacted your mental state. Try to recall those feelings next time you eat for stimulation.

Would it surprise you to know that hyperfocus *and* inattention can be a cause of inconsistent eating patterns? Wait, what? Both? That doesn't seem right. Well, consider this. When you are caught up in hyperfocus mode, do you often catch yourself working for hours without eating? Now flip the coin. When you are distracted (i.e., not being mindful while you are eating), how often have you found, without realizing it, the whole bag of whatever you are snacking on is suddenly gone? No wonder many ADHDers struggle with overeating and binge eating disorder.

Rebecca can attest to this with her nutrition coaching clients. She shared with me that clients of her 10-week coaching program often report binge eating and overeating as their primary problems. In order to work toward healthier habits, these clients work with each other and Rebecca in small groups to share tips and build new habits. One key aspect of her coaching is what Rebecca describes as eating intuitively—recognizing your body's needs and hunger cues and working with them instead of trying to fight them. In addition to the small groups, clients also gain support from a Facebook group, a working group, and a group for ongoing support after the 10 weeks of coaching. Rebecca says group coaching is powerful because you learn from others and their successes, recognize your experience in their stories, and receive validation that you are not the only one with these struggles.

In her experience, some clients need individual guidance too. When working with clients one-on-one, she notes they find tailored solutions to their unique situations helpful because there are many paths to success. It is all about working with people who know how your brain works and trying different approaches until you find what works. If you seek out a coach to help you on your nutrition journey, set up a discovery call with them. Ask them about their approach and mentality surrounding nutrition for ADHDers, and see if you click with them. Coaching is a fabulous tool for neurodiverse leaders, but to make the most of it, you must find a coach that matches your needs and learning style.

ADHDers often need a lot of support to change their eating habits, which may be deeply ingrained from a lifetime of attempting to manage and/or mask their symptoms. If you are not diagnosed until adulthood, you may have developed the habit of using food as a source of dopamine and a coping mechanism for the strong emotions you feel. Remember that is not a bad thing in and of itself. Tools and support systems are available to help achieve balance amid disordered eating habits and allow you to find the right approach to bring out your best as a leader.

Are you asking yourself, "What about meal prepping?" At first glance, it seems it could help solve some of these problems. You're right; it can, *if* meal prepping works for you. Some ADHDers say they use meal prepping to reduce the mental load of deciding what to eat every day (i.e., decision fatigue). It also eliminates the need to cook every day. Who doesn't love that? However, keep in mind that executive functioning challenges make meal-prepping difficult for many ADHDers. The planning, multiple steps, and time/effort required to meal prep regularly can make it challenging for our brains to want to stick to this type of approach over the long term. If you meal prep and it works for you, fantastic! If you don't, there is absolutely nothing wrong with that. Society says that you are just not trying hard enough if you can't adopt habits like meal prepping or restrictive diets. You just don't want to do better. The shame associated with that externally imposed expectation can further erode our ability to succeed. Shake off that shame and focus on what methods work best for you.

You may think, "I am so busy and overwhelmed with work I am not sure how to even begin working on my nutrition." So, we're going to start small. Remember Rebecca's four foundational tips. Eat something every three to four hours, explore other sources of stimulation besides food if you're feeling understimulated or bored, prioritize protein with every meal, and remove the shame in whatever works for you. If that means buying frozen food you can pop into the microwave and out comes fresh steamed green beans, that's great. If that means buying frozen versions of grilled chicken strips, that's fine too. It is about what works for you to achieve a healthy and balanced diet.

We've been talking about tips for success, but how's your overall nutrition knowledge? Before embarking on a journey of what tools may work for you, I want you to understand how much you know about nutrition already. Take this short quiz to see where you're at right now:

1. Can you name the three macronutrients?
2. True or false, fruit has too much sugar and should be avoided.
3. Should you be incorporating protein at every meal?
4. True or false, carbohydrates will make you overweight.
5. How often should you eat throughout the day?

Here are the answers:

1. Proteins, fats and carbohydrates.

2. False. Different fruits have varying levels of natural sugar. Still, they are a valuable source of other nutrients your body needs and can be a great grab-and-go snack, even more so when paired with protein.

3. Yes. Protein is a brain food and the most critical foundational element to your balanced nutrition.

4. False. Incorporating carbohydrates into your nutrition intake will not cause you to become overweight. They are an important macronutrient and great fuel for workouts and muscle building. As long as you eat them in a balanced way with other macronutrients, they will not be the cause of your weight gain.

5. Every 3 to 4 hours while awake. This helps keep you stay satiated, reduces the risk of bingeing, and keeps your brain fueled with what it needs to function optimally throughout the day.

No matter how much you know about healthy eating, you might think, "I have tried and failed at this before. What if I fail again?" No one is perfect. We are often stuck in an all-or-nothing mentality that leads us to believe we are failing if we aren't 110 percent on point. This could not be further from the truth. Remember when we talked about the importance of not being afraid to try again? Keep trying different tactics until you figure out what works best for you. If these tools stop working, try something new. Be flexible and give yourself grace. You've got this.

Move, bitch

In this day and age, I would argue that it is universal knowledge that exercise benefits your body and brain. However, did you know those benefits are even greater for those with ADHD? Movement provides neurotransmitters and hormones that help keep you at the top of your game.

The benefits are backed by research, but just like eating healthy, there are many reasons why ADHD can make it difficult to maintain consistent exercise habits. For example, we may face:

- executive functioning challenges
- time blindness
- overcommitting to other things and feeling like we have no time left for movement
- the all-or-nothing mentality that makes us feel like we're a failure unless we put in massive amounts of time at the gym
- task paralysis.

"What a downer! Why would she start this section with the bad news?" It's not bad! The more you know how your brain works, the better prepared you are to address the challenges head-on. It *is* possible to make exercise a part of your routine, and it will work wonders for your ADHD brain. To be clear, by exercise, I mean moving your body. I am not talking about throwing around ultra-heavy weights or running a marathon. Although, these can be great too if you enjoy doing that. I'm talking about moving in a way that makes you feel good. This can include things as simple as walking your dog, dancing with your kids or doing lunges in your office on your lunch break.

You may feel that exercise is not for you, but it is key to your success with an ADHD brain. Exercise can help manage your ADHD symptoms, giving you an even sharper edge when you take on your day. Exercise produces norepinephrine, dopamine and serotonin, which can help stabilize mood, combat depression, and boost energy and alertness—all things ADHDers struggle with at baseline. It can also reduce stress and improve sleep, mental clarity, self-esteem, social health, and relationships.

You might be thinking, "I have no time for exercise with everything else that's on my plate." Fair point. You are a very busy human. So how much exercise is "enough"? The US Centers for Disease Control and Prevention recommends adults get at least 150 minutes per week of moderate-intensity aerobic activity (CDC 2022). This means you are working hard enough to raise your heart rate and break a sweat, such as brisk walking, water aerobics, or pushing a lawnmower; or 75 minutes per week of vigorous aerobic activity (CDC 2022), such as running, swimming laps, or jumping rope. It's great to spread the exercise throughout the week and incorporate both moderate-intensity and vigorous aerobic activity into the workout routine. For many adults, this means aiming for 30 minutes of exercise five days a week.

Dr. Lauren Grawert is a board-certified addiction psychiatrist and chief of psychiatry for the Northern Virginia service area for the Mid-Atlantic Permanente Medical Group in the United States. She writes:

You can also achieve your weekly activity target with several short sessions of very vigorous intensity activity throughout the week, for example, circuit training, lifting heavy weights, or a mix of moderate, vigorous and very vigorous activity every few days. In general, 75 minutes of vigorous intensity activity a week can give similar health benefits to 150 minutes of moderate activity. If you haven't exercised in a long time, don't worry if you can't reach 150 minutes per week just yet, everyone has to start somewhere. Just set a reachable goal for the day. You can work up towards the recommended amount by increasing your time as you get stronger. Don't let all or nothing thinking keep you from doing what you can every day (Grawert 2021).

Disclaimer: before starting any physical activity or exercise routine, you should consult with your primary care provider to ensure you are safe to do so.

I met with George Eastwood, a certified personal trainer who specializes in neurodiverse clients and is neurodiverse himself. George's story is an inspiring one of introspection and growth. George was diagnosed with Tourette Syndrome at age four. He used sports as a coping mechanism, a masking tool, and a way to increase his confidence and social standing. However, it was not until much later in life that he was diagnosed with ADHD and began to understand why sport and exercise were such foundational elements in his life.

During our conversation, George and I spoke about why he believes exercise is so important for an ADHD brain. He notes that structure and routine can provide a lot of support with ADHD, and exercise is a way to work that structure into your day. Starting your day with movement, even for shorter intervals, like 20 minutes, gives you a sense of a small win. You will experience increased positive thoughts, improved patience, and more motivation to tackle your day.

I asked George what challenges his clients commonly experience and how he combats them. This is his advice:

- Boredom or overwhelm with long workouts or a heavy focus on long-term goals (i.e., significant weight loss, drastic body composition changes, etc.)
  - Break the workouts up into small chunks of time. Intervals with breaks built in can be a great tool for keeping the client engaged without becoming overwhelmed.
- Sensory overload. Some environments, like large gyms or group classes, can be stressful
  - Make sure the environment is supportive. Tailor the approach to meet the client's needs.
- Accountability
  - Having a neurodiverse coach or workout buddy can help keep you accountable and more consistent than if you try to go at it alone.
- Consistency will fluctuate
  - Acceptance and flexibility are the keys to success here. Don't focus on what you did not do, focus on how you can get back on track if you have an off day (or many).

Because exercise provides so many brain benefits, that in and of itself can be a source of motivation for ADHDers when trying to achieve consistency with movement. George said, "You don't just move to get a beach body or a six-pack. You move to improve mental health. Improve the way you think and interact with the world." Isn't that a fabulous and liberating way to look at exercise? Focusing on how you *feel* instead of just how you look. If you look in the mirror every single morning, it will be hard to see the day-to-day changes in your body when you start working out. What will be noticeable from almost day one is your increased focus, better sleep and balanced emotional regulation, improved patience with your family and coworkers, and less stress and anxiety each day. Those are wins worth celebrating.

George identified these three key tips to help you get started:

1. Set clear and honest goals. You want realistic expectations in the short and long term.
2. Have an accountability buddy.
3. Try to do something you enjoy, somewhere you enjoy, with someone you're comfortable with.

With George's advice in mind, I want you to reflect on what types of movement make you happy. Look at the list below and circle the ones that bring you joy.

- Walking
- Running
- Dancing
- Taking the stairs
- Hiking
- Jump rope
- Lifting weights
- Cycling (either in class or outdoors)
- Yoga

- Gymnastics
- Pilates
- Hula hooping
- Soccer
- Tennis
- Basketball
- Hockey
- Pickleball
- Baseball
- Softball
- Rugby
- Football
- Martial arts
- Swimming
- Rock climbing
- Boxing
- Trampolining
- Kayaking
- Paddleboarding
- Axe throwing

A list like this is endless. You might be thinking, "I don't know where to start." Yes, you do. George gave you three actionable tips! Start there. Like Dr. Grawert points out, it is okay to start slow. Aim for 30 minutes of some kind of movement a couple of times a week and then build on that foundation until you reach the goal of 150 minutes of moderate-intensity or 75 minutes of vigorous-intensity aerobic activity per week. Your brain will thank you, and bringing your best self to work will be that much easier.

Hey there, Mr. Sandman

In our next set of "well, that's not fair" facts, did you know that lack of sleep can exacerbate ADHD symptoms? The unfortunate part is that the nature of ADHD can make getting a good night's sleep a challenge. ADHD itself can impact your sleep habits, as can ADHD medication. For argument's sake, let's quantify a "lack of sleep" as less than seven hours on average per night.

I'm not talking about occasional insomnia that plagues most adults. I mean chronic challenges of getting adequate rest. It might seem that you can maintain optimal function with minimal sleep, but I will show you why that is not true. Management and optimization of your ADHD symptoms is your recipe for success. When you lack sleep, your ADHD symptoms worsen, hindering your performance.

Research demonstrates that up to 75 percent of adults with childhood-onset ADHD showed a delayed circadian rhythm phase of an average of 1.5 hours later into the night than healthy non-ADHD adults (Lunsford-Avery and Kollins 2018). Think about the implications of that statistic. Many leaders have a pretty routine work schedule that starts in the morning and ends in the afternoon or evening. However, if you have trouble falling asleep at a time that would allow you adequate rest before you start your workday, this can prove quite problematic.

How can we prove that lack of sleep impacts performance? A 2020 study published in the *Journal of Attention Disorders* compared the effectiveness of completing a continuous performance attention task before and after 25 hours of sustained wakefulness in a controlled environment between participants with and without ADHD (Orrie et al. 2020). Continuous performance tests can measure processes related to vigilance, sustained attention, response inhibition, and other aspects of attention and cognitive function. The study showed that sleep deprivation led to decreased performance across all test variables. However, those with ADHD had more omission and commission errors in completing the continuous performance attention task than their counterparts without ADHD.

ADHD makes it difficult to align with the rest of the world's sleep patterns. It can be tempting to just go without sleep, but lack of sleep can exacerbate your symptoms, and ADHD leaders cannot afford to skip out on sleep. You might think, "It's not my fault. I can't help my challenges with sleep." While you cannot control the wiring of your brain, there are things you can do to facilitate a healthy sleep cycle, even with ADHD. Below, I will share some tips.

What does your nighttime routine look like? To prepare your body for high-quality sleep, try the following steps for good sleep hygiene.

1. Put all electronics, such as your cell phone, smartwatch, tablet, or computer on silent, or turn them off at least 30 minutes before bed. Do not watch TV 30 to 60 minutes before bed.

2. As much as your schedule allows, set a consistent bedtime and stick to it.

3. Keep a notepad or journal by your bed and practice brain dumping during your 30-minute wind down. Write everything down that's in your head. Writing it on paper can release the worry about forgetting important ideas that come to your mind during this time, or upcoming tasks you want to complete.

4. Set out your clothes for the next day. This will eliminate the brain drain of decision-making in the morning and help you relax before bed.

5. Read a book to wind down if that relaxes you. Try to adhere to your bedtime schedule though, and don't get caught up in reading all night.

You might have an inconsistent schedule or think you can't do these things due to the other people you live with and the impact it could have on them. What does it look like to set boundaries for yourself and with others? Could you try adopting these tips one at a time and build on them? These are good sleep hygiene tips for non-ADHDers too; the whole family could benefit from adopting them.

As an added note, chronic lack of sleep can cause many issues in addition to the exacerbation of ADHD symptoms. Talk to your primary care provider if you do not feel that you can regulate your sleep with the tools and tips offered here.

📋 IN SUMMARY

In this chapter, you have learned that caring for your ADHD mind means caring for your body. With ADHD, eating healthy, exercising and getting good sleep can be a challenge. Still, they are crucial to managing your ADHD symptoms and optimizing your leadership performance.

Stop shaming yourself for how you eat, move and sleep right now. Fueling, moving and recharging your body and brain are all a celebration of what your body and brain can do, not a punishment to be endured. Instead, start evaluating your habits. What small changes can you make to sleep, eat and move in ways that make your brain happy and make you a better leader?

Now you know how much the body impacts the ADHD brain. In the next chapter, I will show you how to improve the executive functioning challenges we keep talking about that might be standing in your way.

8

Not Today, Satan. We Put It Off 'Til Tomorrow.

Introduction

Executive dysfunction can make it impossible to maintain a steady and consistent stream of productivity. This can mean missing deadlines, procrastinating on tasks until the last minute, and being unable to effectively multitask when juggling multiple projects. Basically, the opposite of what is expected of most leaders. Ooph! I hate to see it. But you are in luck, you amazing high achiever. I will teach you more about executive function and how to make it your bitch to realize your leadership potential.

Dr. Russell Barkley is an internationally recognized authority on ADHD in children and adults. He has dedicated his career to widely disseminating science-based information about ADHD. Dr. Barkley was previously a professor of Psychiatry and Neurology at the University of Massachusetts Medical Center and a professor of Psychiatry and Health Sciences at the Medical University of

South Carolina. He also taught as a clinical professor of Psychiatry at Virginia Commonwealth University School of Medicine.

In his work, he defined executive functioning challenges in this way:

Individuals with executive dysfunction often struggle to analyze, plan, organize, schedule and complete tasks at all—or on a deadline. They misplace materials, prioritize the wrong things and get overwhelmed by big projects (Barkley 2022).

Everyone has days of minor executive dysfunction, but these challenges consistently plague ADHDers; often to the detriment of our performance as leaders when left unsupported or unmanaged. It might seem like you have juggled everything well enough thus far, but we didn't become leaders to do things "well enough". We want to be exceptional. When you manage your executive functioning skills, you can minimize your stress levels and sense of overwhelm at work. Putting systems into place to help you stay on top of deadlines, tasks, to-do lists, and projects will make you more efficient and effective as a leader.

Executive dysfunction is one of the most challenging parts of ADHD, and it can rear its ugly head in a big way in the workplace. The traditional working world was not built to cater to an ADHD brain or how we work best. This is part of the reason why so many ADHDers choose to become entrepreneurs. But since that path is not for everyone, it is important that we understand how to make our neurodiversity work for us when we work for someone else.

Dr. Scott S. Shapiro is a Harvard Medical School's Massachusetts General Hospital Residency Program graduate, previously the director of Psychiatry at St. Vincent's Catholic Medical School Infectious Disease Center. He is also the founder and director of MilestonesNYC, which matches pro bono mental health providers in New York City to patients in need. He writes, "Executive function tends to be less responsive to medications for adult ADHD compared to the high success rate, 70–80 percent, for other core ADHD symptoms such as focus, hyperactivity, attention, impulsivity, and distractibility. Thus, adults with ADHD continue to experience challenges on the job and in their personal lives" (Shapiro 2019).

His words highlight that no single tool will address every facet of your ADHD presentation. Whether you choose medication or not, you have a responsibility to find and put into place systems that set you up for success. This is especially important for challenges, such as executive functioning, that are less likely to respond to medication. Executive dysfunction impacts your ability to perform many of your responsibilities as a leader—multitasking, meeting deadlines, shifting priorities, and effective analysis and planning. You must find ways that work for you to manage these challenges to reach your peak performance.

Now that we know *why* we must manage our executive dysfunction, we will dive into the *how*. We're going to talk about hyperfocus and how to use it for good, awesome strategies like body doubling and breaking down tasks, and some pretty great tools for keeping your eye on the prize (i.e., effective prioritization), as well as managing impulsivity.

Hyperfocus—superhero or supervillain?

Hyperfocus can be an amazing asset when you need to get things done because it allows us to pay attention to a task, project, interest, etc., in the extreme. You are so dialed in that hours can go by without you noticing. While completing this activity, you lose all track of time and lack conscious awareness of your surroundings. Hyperfocus doesn't just mean paying attention to something for more than two seconds (would you believe that non-ADHDers do this every day??).

Hyperfocus looks like the following:

"I haven't had a sip of water or gotten up to pee in 13 hours because I've been absorbed in what I'm working on, and I had no clue it had even been an hour, never mind 13."

"I stayed up until 4:00 AM researching something that popped into my head at 9:00 PM last night because it was so interesting I couldn't pull myself away."

You all know what I mean. As you're starting to notice these episodes of hyperfocus, It might feel like you can't control them, but the good news is you don't need to control it to make the most of it. The beauty of hyperfocus is that it is often triggered by things we find interesting, fascinating, and/or stimulating. Our brains kick into hyperdrive, trying to consume as much information or complete as much of this interesting task as possible.

Dr. Kathleen Nadeau, a psychologist from Maryland, USA, founder of the Chesapeake Center, and an internationally recognized authority on ADHD, says, "Many scientists, writers and artists with ADHD have had very successful careers in large part because of their ability to focus on what they're doing for hours on end" (as cited in Flippin 2023).

Hyperfocus can allow you to complete a large amount of work in a small amount of time. You are in the zone, and nothing can stop you from attacking whatever project you're fixated on. This can be great when you're pressed for time and juggling multiple priorities. Who wouldn't want to finish a full day's work in a couple of hours? There doesn't seem to be a downside here! A word of caution, if I may: hyperfocus needs to be managed so it does not detract from your performance. If you find yourself hyperfocused on things unrelated to your work, preventing you from completing work on time, or it causes you to neglect your health—not eating, hydrating or using the restroom for most of the day—it might become a hindrance instead of a help.

You might be thinking, "I can't control my hyperfocus. How is it supposed to help me if I can't call it up to the starting line when I need it?" As I mentioned earlier, it does not need to be controlled to be beneficial. Managing it when it occurs is the key to success.

Even if you are hyperfocused on work-related tasks, try to stay as grounded as possible during your workday so you do not miss meetings, appointments, and phone calls because you are laser-focused on the tasks in front of you at that moment. How can you stay grounded? Set alarms for yourself on your phone for upcoming meetings or appointments, or try pop-up calendar reminders on your computer to pull you from your hyperfocused trance. Pay attention to your physical needs too. Make sure you eat every three to four hours, hydrate throughout the day, take stretch breaks at least every hour, and use the restroom as needed.

Hyperfocus episodes can tell you much about your brain and what brings you dopamine. Think about the times you have experienced hyperfocus. Is there anything in common about these episodes? For example, Dr. Nadeau states that she often experiences hyperfocus when tackling a writing project. What tasks or responsibilities bring out your hyperfocus mode?

Use the space below to list your possible hyperfocus triggers.

- _____
- _____
- _____
- _____

How many of these relate to the work you do now? For the ones that relate to your current role, can you schedule these trigger tasks to coincide with the times you need to be most productive?

If you're thinking, "I never experience hyperfocus at work. It's always during non-work times," take a moment to consider this: are you doing work that stimulates you? Are you excited about it? Are you passionate about it? If not, what is keeping you in that line of work?

Since hyperfocus tends to manifest when we do things that interest us, what about the things we *must* do but can't stand? Or the times when we struggle with task initiation in general? Enter body doubling.

Seeing double

Are you familiar with the term body doubling? No, no. It's not the plot of some sci-fi movie about cloning yourself to get more done (although that does sound pretty cool). Body doubling is having another person with you when you have to complete an undesirable task or when you just cannot focus on your own. I am not just talking about another person that is able to physically be in the same room (although if that's possible, that's great). This phenomenon can also be achieved via video calls or chat, such as FaceTime, Zoom, Teams, WebEx, etc.

Having someone just hanging out while you're getting things done might feel silly, but it is a great tool to help kickstart and maintain your productivity. Sometimes you can't wait for the magic of hyperfocus to kick in because certain things need to get done right now. With body doubling, you can accomplish tasks, even boring or annoying ones, without waiting for hyperfocus to arrive.

While there has not been a lot of research into why body doubling works, there is speculation that body doubling is effective because of these five behavioral triggers:

1. Task implementation
2. Social pressure
3. Accountability
4. Specific task direction
5. Activating certain neurotransmitters through behavior.

For example, my twin sister also has ADHD. We'll often FaceTime when we need to do things we don't enjoy, like cleaning or reading a lengthy research article, and we notice a vast improvement in our ability to accomplish everything by having the other person "present" while we work. Whatever the reason, body doubling works and is a great tool to boost your productivity when faced with a task you don't want to do or when you are plagued with distraction.

You might think, "Isn't it less productive to have someone in the room doing the same thing that I am or nothing at all while I'm trying to complete a task? That sounds awkward." That *does* sound awkward! Fear not. The beauty of body doubling is that the other person does not have to be working on the same thing you are. Just having them there makes you more productive. If you need to work on catching up on emails and your body double partner is going to work on the employee schedule, that's great. You can both be working on whatever you need to get done, and you will still be successful.

Consider who might make a good body-doubling partner for you in times of need. You want someone you can work with in person or who works the same hours if you are going to be doing a virtual call. This must be someone that will not distract you— that is key. Can they be silent and independent with their work? They will not be the best choice if they have to pull your focus away to answer their questions or help them with their task. You also want someone you don't feel awkward sharing physical space or a video call with for however long it takes to complete the task at hand. Who comes to mind that might fit this criterion? List them here:

- _____
- _____
- _____
- _____

The idea of asking someone to body double with you can be daunting; however, the benefits to your productivity can be remarkable. Try using this script when approaching your potential body double partner.

"ADHD can make it difficult for me to maintain focus and be productive, even when I must get certain things done. It can be helpful for me to have someone else in the room or on a video chat with me to get into work mode. You can work on whatever you'd like. The key is just having your presence. I won't interrupt your work, and it's helpful if we don't engage other than at scheduled break times. I think this could help me. How do you feel about working together this way, maybe once or twice a week, or whatever schedule works best for you, to see if it would benefit our productivity?"

You might be thinking, "I live alone and work remotely. I don't have anyone that I can body double with." Me too. Hence the FaceTime with my sister, who lives over 1,700 miles away. A body double can be a friend or a family member you don't live with, as long as they don't distract you or attempt to engage with you while you're finishing your work. Utilize whatever method, platform, or app that works for you.

"Ok, Gwen, body doubling sounds great, but sometimes I feel so overwhelmed by what I have to get done that even having someone there doesn't help me get started."

I can completely relate to that. Let me ask you this . . .

How do you eat an elephant?

Breaking big tasks into smaller ones can be a great way to reduce overwhelm and enable you to complete portions over time without leaving the whole thing until the last minute. As the saying goes, that's how you eat an elephant. One bite at a time (not that I would ever recommend you eat an elephant. Please don't do that. They're adorable and so freakin' smart!).

We're talking about those Herculean tasks, right? Like the six-month-long projects with 1,000 stakeholders and one billion tasks to complete along the way? Nope. Well, at least not *just* those. Of course, those big undertakings can be critical, but a task does not have to be big to be overwhelming. You can break up small tasks too, if it helps you get started. Breaking down your projects might feel challenging, but I will show you some helpful steps and tools.

If you are overwhelmed by the scale of the task at hand, you can be trapped in task paralysis (the state of knowing all the things you need to do but being unable to get started on any of them. Despite the fact that your brain is screaming at you to get something done, you cannot get going). This can result in missing deadlines or subpar results. By breaking tasks down, you can stay on top of them and deliver your best work on time.

In one of my leadership roles, I was made responsible for opening a robotic operating room in the labor and delivery unit. I had three months from start to finish to check off:

- the completion of the renovation work that was needed within the space
- recruiting and training a new team to staff the area
- planning for how this operating room workflow would achieve safe and seamless integration into the already established labor and delivery workflow
- getting the physicians and staff excited about the idea
- making sure all of the equipment, instrumentation, supplies, etc., were in place before the ribbon cutting.

All of that in 90 days. Yikes. I was fortunate enough to have a good friend at that job who had already developed a project management tracker template. This served as a framework we could fill out with each step needed to be completed and all of the people who needed to be looped in. Many apps will do this now too—Trello, Asana, ClickUp, Wrike, Active Collab, Airtable, GoodDay, Jira, etc.

As I was new to large-scale project management at the time, I stuck with the template tracker my colleague had provided, and it worked wonders for keeping everyone on track and on the same page. We launched on time and developed a successful robotic program because we could break this gargantuan task down into manageable bite-size pieces. That robotic program is still running strong over four years later. You eat an elephant just like you would eat an apple, one bite at a time. Break down your tasks into manageable steps to help you stay on track and avoid overwhelm.

You might be thinking, "Even the idea of breaking down a task into steps is overwhelming." Try calling in the cavalry. Think of someone you can partner with to help you identify which project areas can be pieced out and put into a tracking template. To start breaking down a task on your to-do list, ask yourself the following questions:

- What can I accomplish in under five minutes? For example, sending an email to set up a meeting with a stakeholder.
- What can I accomplish in a day? For example, connecting with vendors and getting a list of the equipment you need.
- What can I accomplish in a week? For example, holding staff meetings for all your team members to elicit project feedback and address any objections or concerns.

If you don't have a tracking template at your disposal, you can use tools like a Gantt chart (mock example shown below) that can be created in Excel, or apps like Canva, ClickUp, and Wrike if you don't want to create your own.

You might think, "I don't have the time to break things down. This timeline is too tight, and it all needs to get done *right now*." In that case, think about what you can delegate and to whom you feel confident delegating. If there is no way you can accomplish everything that the task requires in the time you are given, outsource as much as you can to team members that you trust.

Writing This Book

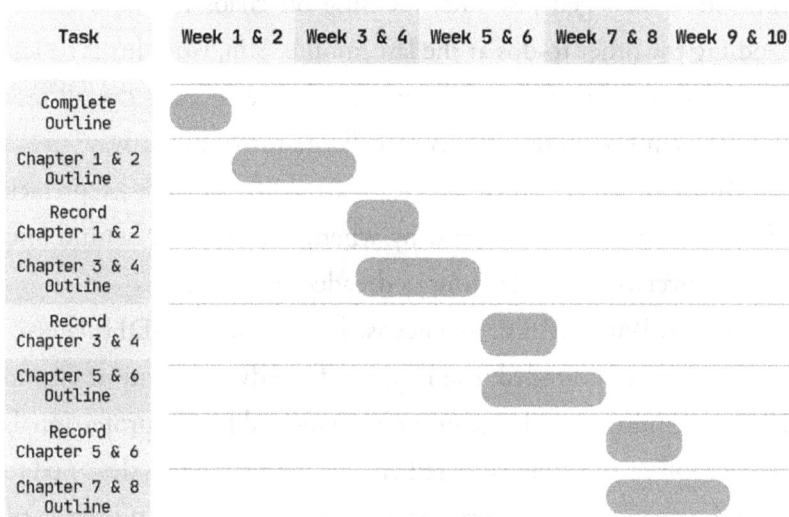

Task	Week 1 & 2	Week 3 & 4	Week 5 & 6	Week 7 & 8	Week 9 & 10
Complete Outline	▰				
Chapter 1 & 2 Outline	▰				
Record Chapter 1 & 2		▰			
Chapter 3 & 4 Outline		▰			
Record Chapter 3 & 4			▰		
Chapter 5 & 6 Outline			▰		
Record Chapter 5 & 6				▰	
Chapter 7 & 8 Outline				▰	

These tools are great for each project, but what about keeping track of my priorities and to-do list on a larger scale? Time to show me your war face.

Let's go to war

When you are always putting out fires and dealing with the latest chaos, keeping track of your priorities as an ADHD leader can be difficult. Start by thinking, "What is a 'must do' versus a 'can do' if I have the time?" It's important to know this distinction. I am not saying that putting out fires or dealing with chaos should go on the back burner. There will be unexpected situations that require immediate attention; they are just par for the course as a leader. I want to make sure we set you up with tools so you don't lose track of your running priority list of everything *other* than chaos. It might seem like you've managed just fine, focusing on chaos first and always handling the other to-dos at the last minute. Still, wouldn't it be less stressful to feel like you can be more effective in your overall task management no matter what curveballs are thrown your way?

Multitasking is a must as a leader, but if you can't keep track of what needs to be done and by when, you will fall behind and become overwhelmed, leading to dreaded task paralysis.

Andrew Bordt, M.Ed., is a licensed educator and ADHD entrepreneur who co-founded The Institute for Advancement of Group Therapy. Andrew and his team provide mental health professionals with a toolbox of evidence-based engagement strategies designed to meet the needs of diverse groups, maximizing growth and recovery, and capital skill-building for everyone in the room, even those with ADHD. Their mission is to help more people heal and improve patient outcomes. Right after I was diagnosed with ADHD and I shared my diagnosis on LinkedIn, Andrew reached out, even though he did not know me. He offered to chat with me about his experience and offer guidance. He has overcome some incredible challenges in his life, and his passion for helping others is evident. Andrew shared with me that he chooses to manage his ADHD without medication. This has motivated him to develop and implement some great tools for staying on-task and well-organized as he works through shifting priorities as a co-founder.

Of the tools that we discussed, my personal favorite was the "war board". This time management strategy comes from Andrew's time working for The Walt Disney Company. It is also referred to as the Eisenhower or Priority Matrix. Andrew says tools, like a war board, helped him better manage the stress associated with ADHD and minimized some stress-causing behaviors.

Here's how Andrew taught me to set up my war board:

1. Divide a piece of paper into four quadrants.
2. Label the left column 'important' and the right 'nominal'.
3. Label the top row 'urgent' and the bottom row 'not pressing'.
4. From there, sorting daily tasks using sticky notes is easy.

Of course, this can also easily be done on a phone or computer, but I like the tactile aspect of the paper configuration, and it's very satisfying to rip off a task once it's complete. I also recommend focusing on one task at a time and silencing phones and email notifications until it's finished. Then, if a critical and urgent task arises, simply re-evaluate and, if necessary, rearrange the board.

As Andrew points out, the items on your board can and should be moved around as your priorities shift. As a leader or entrepreneur, your priorities are always changing. It can be easy to lose track of what is most important or what is due when. Tools like this are a great way to keep on top of your game and deadlines.

You might think, "It is rare that I am in my office. This strategy wouldn't work for me because it's not easy to access on the go." If you're always on the go, remember you can make a mini-war board on your phone. It can be recreated in a Note or a Word document easily, so you can still manage priorities wherever you are. If you need multiple people engaged in the priority tracking, you can create a shared space like the boards available on Miro, an online platform that allows you and your team to connect, collaborate and co-create in a shared space (miro.com).

How are you going to set up your version of a war board? Will you use it as described or add a personal touch? If you have an office setting or somewhere you frequent during the workday, set up a physical board and pick up color-coded markers or sticky notes. If you are always on the go, set one up on your phone, tablet, or laptop.

Here's an example of a war board I created:

	Important	Nominal
Urgent	Send digital education materials and tracking spreadsheet to Morgan. Create and submit expense report for the last two weeks. Publish the next schedule block for employees.	Go to mail room to check department mail. Return call to vendor and approve scheduled in-servicing for next week. Email service line Vice President to confirm leader rounding schedule.
Not Pressing	Schedule a meeting with manager and assistant manager for check in two weeks. Write five employee thank you cards. Put together an agenda for supervisor meeting next month to send out for approval.	Get a quote from vendor for new desk chairs for employees. Call documentation shredding company to schedule a pickup of shred boxes. Call maintenance to hang the coat board in my office.

You might think it will be hard to keep up with this new system as you adapt. Don't beat yourself up. Most tools cannot be fully adopted overnight with immediate success. Don't let that deter you. Do what you can until it becomes a habit. If the war board doesn't work for you, don't be afraid to try other tactics, such as setting calendar alarms on your phone for upcoming deadlines or blocking your calendar out for things you must get done without distraction. Remember Chapter Six: If at first you don't succeed . . . try, try again.

So far, we've talked about all things "task completion", but did you know impulsivity is also a component of executive dysfunction?

Impulsivity insight

Being impulsive is not always a bad thing. Sometimes it can lead to fantastic life changes or great breakthroughs, but it also has the potential to go rogue and wreak havoc. Being impulsive means you don't do much (or any) thinking before you say or do certain things. Of course, everyone is impulsive sometimes, but as discussed in Chapter Two, for ADHDers, it can be the baseline. It may seem like being impulsive has paid off big for you—I'm sure in some ways it has—but as leaders, we need to manage our impulsivity to avoid negative consequences.

When you consistently exhibit impulsive behavior, you risk big losses, derailed projects or inappropriate communication. Think back to the hissy fit I threw in that leadership training. Impulsivity can be positive, but you must take appropriate steps to ensure it is well-managed and put to good use.

Remember Brooke Schnittman, our friend that owns her own ADHD coaching company? She cites an ADHDer's ability to jump into things headfirst without knowing everything about it as a reason why we can succeed as entrepreneurs. We take the idea of "there will never be a right time, so we may as well do it now" and run with it.

Many of the ADHD entrepreneurs and leaders I know have started something without ever knowing what they were doing. They were confident that they could learn along the way. Take Leah Turner, for example. She is a LinkedIn trainer and ADHDer who leads corporate and group training, runs digital courses, and performs public speaking. At the time of writing, she has almost 170,000 followers and made over €600,000 in revenue in her first 3 years on LinkedIn. She says,

> I'd never received any training before I hosted my first LinkedIn session. I'd never taken a digital course before I built my own. I'd never been to a workshop before I created and delivered workshops. I'd only been to one speaking event before I started speaking at events. Some may call that stupid, some may say I was ill prepared, but with no knowledge of how other people do things, no one to copy . . . I developed a style all my own, a way that is authentic to me and my brand and honestly, it's going pretty well. Overpreparation can kill your individuality and dull what makes you unique. Don't do everything the way you've seen other people do it. Be brave enough to do things your way and take a risk. Your way might be better (Turner 2022).

Impulsivity is a great tool for success for ADHDers when we make room for safety nets and steer clear of chaos whenever possible. Just like with hyperfocus, you may think, "I can't control when I'm impulsive. How do you expect me to direct it into just positive projects or ideas?" It may be too lofty of a goal to say that we will *always* use our impulsivity for good and not evil, but this is why it's important to set up guardrails for yourself. Mitigate as much risk as possible to give yourself the best odds for a good outcome!

I'll give you an example. I've told you I'm horrible with money and sometimes spend too much. Other than working with a financial advisor who pulls money from my account every month, I also take steps like keeping credit cards tied up in plastic wrap and packing tape in a drawer at home so I don't have unfettered access to them. The forced pause of cutting open packing tape and plastic wrap to get to credit cards helps me think, "Do I really need to be buying this?" Impulsivity can be managed so that when it does show up, it shows up to serve us, not hold us back.

Let's relate this back to you. What is an idea that you have been sitting on because you are worried you don't know enough or you aren't prepared? For example, this could be a suggestion for optimizing workflows, improving efficiency or even an idea for your own company or service. Take this idea and complete the chart below. (Side note: you can also use this chart for all areas that impulsivity might impact, such as excessive spending. How might you complete the chart to manage your credit card usage?)

The idea	Positive intended results	Potential negative outcomes	Safety net(s) to mitigate the negatives

You might think, "If I fail or make a bad suggestion, it could mean risking my job." That is why it's important to consider what could go wrong and what safety nets could be put in place to minimize the risks. If you are not supported to try new and innovative things at work, I challenge you to consider this, can you ever feel confident that this environment supports who you are as an ADHD leader?

📋 IN SUMMARY

In this chapter, you have learned that executive functioning and its components can be challenging at work. But with the right tools, support systems and guardrails in place, these challenges can be overcome and conquered. You now know that hyperfocus can be used as a springboard for productivity instead of a shackle that holds you back from getting the most important things done.

Enlisting a trusted partner to body double with can help get you on track. Tasks large and small that used to feel very overwhelming can be tackled by breaking them down into smaller steps to reduce anxiety and task paralysis. Multitasking does not have to be your nemesis now that you have tools and tips for maintaining constant oversight of your priorities and to-do list, no matter how much the items shift around. Even your impulsivity can be a great tool in your leadership strategy because you know ways to manage it productively, which will benefit you more than harm you.

Please stop shaming yourself for the executive function struggles that you have. You are not lazy or stupid. Your brain is different in its inner workings; there is nothing wrong with that. Start using your ADHD to your advantage as a leader—the gifts it gives you can be your biggest strengths. I want you to start identifying which of the tools in this chapter you can implement to avoid any of the downsides of unmanaged ADHD symptoms. Tailor them to meet your needs and fit your life. Put them to work for you!

Now you know how to begin conquering your executive functioning challenges and optimize your brain functioning for peak leadership performance. In the next chapter, I will show you how you can optimize your emotions as an ADHD leader and use them to benefit you, your team, and your business.

9

Emotions Are Not Your Enemy

Introduction

The strong emotions associated with ADHD can result in emotional displays that are considered disruptive or unprofessional in many work settings. To combat this, you may have developed masking techniques to suppress these displays. However, masking can be difficult to maintain over the long term because it is an act instead of an expression of our true self. It takes a lot of work to "keep up appearances" and can be exhausting. On top of the energy it requires, masking may not even have the intended effect. You may be perceived as cold or insensitive in your attempts to remain even-keeled. On the opposite end of the spectrum, you may lose control—like it or not, here it comes. Blowing up in anger or breaking down into sobbing fits because you can only suppress your feelings for so long before they force themselves to the surface. As a result, you are left frustrated with yourself and the situation. You want to be "professional", but it feels like trying to walk a tightrope while balancing ten elephants on your back. Sooner or later, you and those elephants will come crashing down.

While this book is intended for all leaders, I would be remiss if I did not point out that women have long struggled with being perceived as too emotional. This perception carries across our personal and professional lives and applies to neurodiverse and non-neurodiverse individuals alike. In a 2020 study by Marshburn et al., in *Frontiers in Psychology* titled "Workplace Anger Costs Women Irrespective of Race", the authors found that women who expressed anger in the workplace were rated as the least competent when compared to women who expressed sadness and men who expressed either anger or sadness. Challenges with emotional regulation in ADHD can exacerbate this struggle. This means the chances are even greater that we will be perceived as incompetent professionals and leaders. We can be held back from reaching our full potential as a result. Overall this negative correlation between emotions and competence has been a larger problem for women. Still, men with ADHD also struggle with emotional regulation. They too may experience a negative impact on how their competency is perceived based on their ability to regulate emotions at work. With an ever-increasing focus on emotional intelligence in leadership, being perceived as lacking control over our emotional expression can hinder every one of us on our journey as leaders.

In addition to finding an environment and people that are supportive of you, there are ways to help make sure your emotions are a source of strength for you as a leader. In this chapter, we talk about "strong" emotions or emotional displays. When I say "strong", I mean in comparison to your neurotypical counterparts. The way you express your feelings is normal for you; however, these expressions can be perceived as excessive in the workplace, depending on the environment and the people you work with.

Some people equate masking with behaving professionally. This is incorrect. Masking your emotions, behaviors, tendencies, communication, etc. does not mean just trying to behave professionally. Instead, it is the act of forcing yourself to behave, react, and communicate in ways that are inauthentic to your ADHD brain (i.e., mimicking the behaviors of your neurotypical peers). It might feel like your emotions are your enemy, but they can be a differentiator for you as a leader. In this chapter, I will show you how to flip that switch.

In the early chapters of this book, I described what emotional dysregulation can feel and look like and how we cope with it. Let's take a look at some research on this. A 2020 study by Thorell et al., published in the *Journal of Clinical and Experimental Neuropsychology*, titled "Emotion Dysregulation in Adult ADHD: Introducing the Comprehensive Emotional Regulation Inventory (CERI)" revealed that adults with ADHD are more likely than their neurotypical counterparts to use the less effective emotional regulation strategies of situational avoidance or emotional suppression when faced with emotionally challenging situations.

Emotional suppression (hiding one's emotions from others) is described as a less advanced strategy for regulating emotions than other methods. Situational avoidance (avoiding situations in which strong or challenging emotions may occur) can be a recipe for disaster if not managed delicately. Leaders cannot avoid *all* the people and situations that may cause us to experience strong emotions. This is often where our most important work gets done.

The authors of this study cite attentional deployment (diverting your attention away from an emotional situation), and reappraisal (interpreting the situation in an alternative way to reduce strong emotions) as more advanced emotional regulation strategies that are implemented less often in the ADHD group versus the control group. The study notes that one possible reason for this trend is what is called temporal discounting—when those with ADHD prioritize short-term benefits over long-term goals. One statement from the study struck me immediately: ". . . patients with ADHD reported significantly more problems implementing strategies for regulating emotions as well as a higher negative impact of emotional dysregulation on daily life" (Thorell et al. 2020).

Great. So we know it is a big problem, and we have a more challenging time doing something about it. Time to give up! Ha. Nice try, but you're not getting off that easy. Emotional regulation is an almost universal challenge among ADHDers, but your emotions are not your enemy. Differing presentations of emotional expression between ADHD and non-ADHD leaders are not negative and do not have to hinder performance. Your strong emotions can be a cornerstone to your success when provided with the right environment and support.

In this chapter, we will talk about the differences in emotional expression and regulation between those with ADHD and those without. I will show you how to put your passion to work, find healthy outlets, and seek support systems for improving how others perceive you professionally. I will also touch on how these things can enhance your personal relationships as well.

Hysteria!

Emotional dysregulation is no picnic (or if it were, it would be pouring rain, and your food would be covered in ants). One minute you are doing fine and in a great mood; the next, you are sobbing or screaming without warning. It is frustrating and confusing for you and often the people around you. It may also present a less-than-flattering picture of who you are as a leader. Think of this aspect of ADHD as less like a battle and more like a roller-coaster. You will have your ups and downs, but you can find a way to enjoy the ride. I will show you some ways to get there in a bit. Hang tight.

According to Cohen et al. (2021) in their study titled "Emotional Dysregulation and Health Related Quality of Life in Young Adults with ADHD: A Cross Sectional Study", from *Health and Quality of Life Outcomes*, emotional dysregulation is the inability to modify your emotional state to promote adaptive, goal-oriented behaviors. For leaders with ADHD, this goes beyond occasional bouts of stress or overwhelm. It is constant and often unpredictable fluctuations in mood that may not seem to match the situation in ways deemed appropriate (based on neurotypical norms or expectations). It may feel like your emotions will always hold you back, so you must mask, suppress (push your feelings and emotions down instead of expressing them), or avoid (pretend your emotions do not exist and neglect to address them at all).

But none of these are healthy options in the short or long term. Once you learn how to navigate your emotions and display them in productive ways, they can be rocket fuel for your development as a leader. In leadership, appearances are everything. When you can navigate the different ways your emotions show up at work, you can maintain a strong executive presence and inspire confidence in your leadership abilities.

In my second director position, I had the gold standard of a supportive and empathetic leader. (We're talking about Bonnie from Chapter Five, of course.) She does not have ADHD. While working for her, I did not know I had it either. Neither of those things mattered. Bonnie recognized early on that my emotions were powerful and sometimes unpredictable. During our time together, she supported me in expressing my emotions fully and authentically; in the appropriate settings. Often this meant sitting in her office or talking to her on the phone to work through frustrations (read: screaming swear words and venting). Other times, I was overcome by frustration and just had to cry it out to her always in-tune listening ear.

Because I was able to process my real feelings in a safe space, when the time came for meetings and executive presentations, I was prepared to approach the situation with more level emotions. In addition to keeping me out of trouble, this set the stage for my positive emotions to shine. My passion and enthusiasm for my work were front and center because Bonnie supported me in working through the negative feelings without judgment or reprisal. As a leader with ADHD, your emotions are stronger and can be more unpredictable, but they do not have to be your enemy. Learning to recognize, honor and process them without masking, suppressing or avoiding them will allow you to show up as your authentic self while highlighting your strengths as a leader. It is critical that you find places and people with whom you can feel safe expressing your emotions. If you don't, unmasking will be an uphill battle at best and, at worst, impossible.

You might think, "I never seem to know when my emotions will fluctuate, which makes it challenging for me to stop them from coming out or hit the pause button in time." The whole point is not to stop them from coming. It's to make sure we can express them in healthy and productive ways. We will discuss healthy outlets in a later section, but don't forget, emotions are not your enemy. No matter how often you have been told they are unprofessional or not aligned with leadership potential, that is not true.

Think back to the last time you were told you were "too emotional" or received negative feedback based on how you display your emotions as a leader. Did that situation cause you to want to mask, suppress, or avoid your feelings even more? On what occasions did employing those strategies work for you? When do these strategies fail or fall short? Emotions don't go away just because we ignore them or try to push them down. That often makes them worse. You need to get to know your feelings and your triggers so you can process them in productive ways when they occur.

Think about the last five instances where you had an emotional display of anger, sadness, or any other feeling at work that your colleagues perceived as negative. Then, fill out the chart below using the first row as an example.

Situation/trigger	Your response	Their reaction
You're informed you have to attend training. The training title gives the impression you will now be responsible for taking on additional responsibilities that currently fall within another department's scope.	You bring your concern to HR, expressing your frustration that there was no prior communication and that it seems you have to assume ownership over a struggling process instead of the current responsible party being held accountable for their performance.	You are told you should have brought this to your manager first instead of HR and that the training was an expensive opportunity the company invested in for employee development. A week later, an email states that the training has been rescheduled. It further explains that it is for your development, not an assumption of additional responsibility.

Situation/trigger	Your response	Their reaction

This exercise aims to build awareness of the situations that may trigger you. It can help you identify how others may react to your emotional responses. You may have been suppressing, masking, and avoiding for so long that you don't know where to start. This is the area where I recommend calling in the cavalry. A therapist, psychologist or psychiatrist can be invaluable in guiding you on your journey of healthy emotional processing and displays.

If you are currently seeing a mental healthcare provider, do they have any experience in treating ADHD? If not, see if they would be willing to brush up on the latest research to be better prepared to help you in this area. If you are not seeing someone now, what's stopping you? (This question is meant for reflection, not judgment or shaming. I only want to help you get set up with the resources you need to make you successful.)

Putting your passion to work

ADHDers excel when they are doing what they love. While that is true for most people, it is even more notable when you have our type of neurodiversity. Despite the name, ADHD is not an issue of a *deficit* of attention. It is a difficulty in the equal application of attention across the board. ADHDers are excellent at taking on the new and exciting, as well as anything that interests us. But we can experience significant struggles with tasks that don't stimulate or engage us. This can be used to your advantage. Doing things that stimulate our brain and give us dopamine increases the production of our brain's happy chemicals. We could all use more happy. So, put your passion into working and finding ways to spend less time on things that do not stimulate your brain. This will help set the tone for more balanced emotions.

When you, as an ADHDer, are disengaged or not passionate about your work, you cannot "power through" the boring stuff with relative ease as non-ADHDers can. Passion is paramount. Now, I don't mean to say that you must love every second of every day at work. If you have found that, call me and tell me your secret. For most of us, the reality is that we will have good and bad days. The key is that you are leading in a way that allows you to focus on your passions and keeps you operating at your best.

It might feel like a pipe dream to find a job that will stimulate, engage, and support the *real* you over the long term when you have ADHD, but don't give up hope. So many ADHDers I know found their calling later in life (e.g., moving from finance to public speaking or technology to operations). Maybe they never dreamed how much they could love their new industry. However, they found their passion in being authentic to themselves and exploring what kept them interested and engaged. I also like to point out that it is ok (and somewhat common for ADHDers) to have multiple callings across the lifespan. Moving from role to role or industry to industry can allow you to gain so much experience and fulfillment. Each role may serve you for different reasons at different points in your life, which is wonderful! That's one of the beautiful things about ADHD. You have the potential for so much passion. Your job is to ensure it is put to good use—in the right environment and for the right people.

As you know from earlier chapters, ADHD brains are quick to experience boredom. They must be stimulated in the right ways in order to stay engaged. Emphasizing the part of your leadership role that you are most passionate about will help further highlight your strengths. It is also a great reason to aspire to leadership in the first place. In leadership and entrepreneurial roles, you may have more control over how you work and what you work on.

The biggest passion for me within leadership is the people. There is no greater feeling than elevating others and helping them reach their potential, beyond what they can fathom for themselves. Even in my most stressful and overwhelming times as a leader, bringing myself back to the people was what kept me going.

I spoke earlier in a previous chapter about the bonds and connections I made with our teams. I still find that to be my biggest driving force in leadership. My best work was done when collaborating with our people. My lasting relationships with them prove that living and leading with passion will result in success. Your passion is a massive strength with ADHD. You can pour so much into your leadership role when you focus on what drives you and stimulates your brain to be and stay engaged.

Are you wondering, "Doesn't unchecked passion come across as unprofessional?" As long as passion is demonstrated in productive ways (i.e., don't be as "passionate" as I was in voicing my displeasure with that tardy trainer because . . . yikes), it should always be celebrated as a strength. If your current leadership environment does not support you to express your passions and focus your work around them, how long do you think you will be able to stay engaged and produce your best work?

When I say passion through the lens of leadership, what is the first thing that comes to mind? Which parts of your role do you adore? Which do you abhor? Fill in the list below with your top three passions as a leader. How much of your current role centers around these passions? What can you do to put more focus on these moving forward?

1. _____
2. _____
3. _____

Here are some tips for how to express passion professionally.

- Express negative emotions in a safe time and place and with a safe person.
  - For example, I adopted the tactic of getting up to use the restroom if I felt myself getting too angry or

upset during meetings. Taking this approach allowed me to remove myself from the situation to regroup in a non-disruptive way. It did not draw negative attention toward me or raise any concerns about why I was leaving the room. No one questioned it, and this tactic allowed me the time I needed to get back to a level head and return to the meeting.

- Express your passion for your work in a positive way, and be upfront.
  - For example, "I am very passionate about improving the morale and satisfaction of our team. If I come across as emotional or inappropriate, it is because I care about these outcomes on a deep level. I am committed to being part of the solution. I would love to work together to find a way to achieve the team's goals without sacrificing the wellbeing of our staff."

Maybe you're someone that doesn't feel very passionate about any parts of your current role. Maybe whatever you were passionate about has since fizzled out and doesn't excite you anymore. If that's the case, spend time reflecting. Can you make any changes in your current role to bring your previous passions to a place where you feel reinvigorated and re-energized? What about your passions outside of work? Can you explore any of these as a career? Once you have identified these passions, put together actionable steps to reshape your current role or find a new one to better align with what you love and are best at.

Chasing catharsis

Finding healthy outlets for your emotions is critical when you have ADHD. By using the right emotional expression tools, you can smooth out some of the stomach-turning ups and downs of your rollercoaster. Healthy outlets are whatever works for you to process emotions in a non-self-destructive and cathartic way. I don't mean just the quintessential advice of doing yoga, although that can do wonders for you if you are into that sort of thing. Have you seen the classes they offer where you can do yoga with puppies and baby goats? Count me in for all of that! But I digress.

There is a multitude of outlets through which you can achieve cathartic emotional expression. Let's go to the opposite end of the spectrum from puppies and baby goats but stick with the theme. Have you ever heard of rage yoga? This "alternative yoga for the modern badass" founded by Lindsay Istace, can involve heavy metal guitar riffs, f-bombs, war cries, dirty jokes, and even alcohol consumption. I've never tried it, but I won't lie; that sounds like my kind of yoga. Of course, I am not trying to say that some form of yoga is the only answer. Baby animals and obscenity-laced war cries just seem like an excellent way to remind you that the spectrum of options is almost limitless. It all depends on what is cathartic for you.

It might feel like you have tried everything and are still struggling with healthy outlets, but that's okay. We will discuss options to shake off the shame and put you on a path to success. ADHDers are at a much higher risk of developing unhealthy coping mechanisms—think alcohol, nicotine, substance abuse, and binge eating, etc. This risk increases when you are diagnosed late in life. By finding emotional outlets that lift you up instead of holding you back, you can realize exponential growth in your leadership potential.

I have struggled my entire life with unhealthy coping mechanisms. I have always had an unhealthy relationship with food and battle binge eating disorder. I also used to smoke cigarettes and drink one or two too many. A couple of years ago, I hit a point where I wanted things to be different, so I signed up with a nutrition and fitness coach and hit the ground running. I was eating clean, working out five days a week, and I felt fabulous. Chapter Seven discussed the benefits of healthy eating, physical activity, and good sleep for ADHDers. Through movement and improving my health, I found a cathartic emotional outlet.

Sometimes this meant crying at the gym or yelling out loud if I missed a lift, but that's okay. Sometimes it meant listening to heavy metal music at full volume and lifting heavy weights to blow off steam. Overall, it meant that I could better manage stress at work and smooth out my emotional undulations because of the happy brain chemicals that my lifestyle provided. It was the safe space for my body to do whatever it needed to do in the moment, whether it be cry, scream, laugh, or celebrate. Healthy emotional outlets are a foundational element to authentic leadership with ADHD while minimizing the potential for negative emotional expression to derail you at work.

You might be saying to yourself, "I find it so hard to maintain interest in exercising and eating healthy all the time." That was just an example. I mentioned that ADHD tools are fluid and we should always try, try again. The idea is to find something that works for you until it doesn't and then find something else. If exercise is not an effective emotional outlet for you, that's ok. It is still an important tool for optimizing ADHD but it does not have to be your primary outlet. Maybe it's art. Maybe it's music. Maybe it's being in nature. Maybe it's screaming into a pillow or sobbing into that same pillow until it is soaked. Whatever you do should be cathartic and productive toward your goals whenever possible, not self-destructive or self-sabotaging.

What are your current methods for processing difficult emotions? How do those methods impact your emotional state in the short and long term? How do they further your abilities to perform as a leader? List your four go-to coping mechanisms when strong emotions arise, and check off whether you would categorize them as helping or hindering you in pursuing your goals. Again, this is not to shame or judge. Instead, it is to help you recognize areas you might want to focus on.

Coping mechanism	Helping	Hindering
e.g. excessive alcohol consumption		×
e.g. taking a walk outside	×	

Breaking from long-standing coping mechanisms can be a challenge, even when we know they are doing more harm than good. "I have tried to make these healthy changes before. It's so much easier to stick with what I know." Trust me when I say I empathize with you there. Eating healthy and working out five days a week is not my current reality. I have fallen off the "healthy wagon" more times than I can count, and sometimes that wagon gets miles away before I can even start to chase it again. This is a journey, and every step counts. Think back to the tools we talked about in the last chapter. Can you use body doubling or calendar blocking to incorporate healthier habits or coping mechanisms into your day?

Seek support

Humans are pack animals. As a general rule, we are not meant to go at this life alone. With ADHD and neurodiversity as a whole, this is even more important. ADHDers crave connection. It is crucial to your success to find the right tribe of people to support you in your leadership journey and who encourage you to leverage your ADHD brain. I don't just mean other neurodiverse people, although it can be of tremendous help to have at least a couple in your circle to relate to. Your tribe can (and should) be composed of people that are going to make you a better leader. These can be friends, family, colleagues, leaders above and around you, therapists or healthcare workers, and even respectful dissenters. Whoever helps lift you up and develops you into your best self falls into this category.

It may feel like you have all the support you need, but how much is tailored to your unique experience as an ADHD leader? You may struggle to hit your stride at work without a strong support system. As a result, you could be left feeling as though you are stagnating instead of progressing. The right people in your corner will help you achieve your potential by supporting you to maximize your ADHD assets.

My tribe has changed as I've gotten older, and that has a lot to do with the fact that even before I knew I had ADHD, I always knew something was different about me. I had specific needs. The truest supporters on my leadership journey encouraged me to reach for new heights, believe in myself when all I had were doubts, and chase the dreams that meant the most to me as an ADHD leader. Without their guidance and support, I would never have written this book or founded the END Institute. You can achieve a lot on your own, but having the right tribe around you can take you places you may have never thought possible.

Seeking the right kind of support will pave your path to success. You are not in this alone. You might think, "I don't know if I'm comfortable enough yet to talk openly about my ADHD. How can I find people who will support me if I prefer to keep this to myself?" Think about the people who have supported you—not the fickle or fair-weather friends, but the people who strive to understand the good, the bad, and the ugly—and want to help you improve. Bonnie and I never had a conversation about ADHD when I worked for her, and yet she has been one of the most supportive and formative forces in my life to date.

I would also encourage you to join my END Institute community (contact information at the back of the book). You can be as active or passive in your engagement as you want in discussions led by ADHD professionals and leaders. You might be surprised by how comforted you find yourself when surrounded by people that know what you're going through.

Support looks different for everyone. Before figuring out how to find supportive people, you need to know what support means to you. Use the space below to list all the things that are critical for you to have in a supportive member of your tribe. For example, they could be empathetic, compassionate, or able to have deep conversations instead of just chit-chat.

- _____
- _____
- _____
- _____
- _____
- _____
- _____
- _____

Does anyone in your life fit this profile now? If not, where do you think you might find someone like this? What types of activities or environments could you align yourself with that may expose you to more people that belong in your tribe? For example, it could be a young leaders' educational summit, an ADHD conference, or collaboratives like the END Institute.

You might push back here and say, "I don't want to cut people out of my life that don't fit that list." I get that. As always, you are the only person who can decide how much or how little influence someone has in your life. My mission is to help you reach your goals by giving you the tools to identify the types of people that will support you the most on your leadership journey. Who you decide to keep or to cut will forever be your choice.

Better me, better we

As I mentioned previously, personal relationships and ADHD can be a book all of its own. But I want to take a brief moment to point out that understanding and harnessing our emotions does not only benefit us, but those around us. We improve personal relationships when we acknowledge, embrace and seek to optimize our emotions—using them to strengthen our connections with other people. I don't just mean romantic relationships. Personal relationships can include friends, family, or even colleagues you connect with on a different level.

It might seem like personal relationships don't have anything to do with leadership potential, but in Chapter Three, we spoke about the impacts that personal relationships can have on your professional life. Every successful leader, ADHD or not, will thrive on emotional support from partners and friends. If you have struggled to find and maintain healthy friendships or relationships in the past, don't give up. Instead, see it as part of your overall leadership toolkit.

By improving your personal relationships, you strengthen your support system, self-awareness, and ability to perform at your peak at work. How so? Well, because you have minimized a source of outside stress. A 2022 study by Gronewold and Engles published in *Frontiers in Integrative Neuroscience* titled "The Lonely Brain – Associations Between Social Isolation and (Cerebro-) Vascular Disease From the Perspective of Social Neuroscience" points out that neurodiverse individuals "experience loneliness and negative social contact much more than neurotypicals, despite longing for social contact. They report many barriers to socializing and that socializing with neurotypicals can be exhausting, challenging or anxiety-provoking".

CHADD (Children and Adults with Attention-Deficit/Hyperactivity Disorder) points out in the section on their website titled, 'Relationships & Social Skills' that:

Individuals with ADHD often experience social difficulties, social rejection and interpersonal relationship problems as a result of their inattention, impulsivity and hyperactivity. Such negative interpersonal outcomes cause emotional pain and suffering. They can also appear to contribute to the development of comorbid mood and anxiety disorders (CHADD 2018).

Emotional pain, suffering, and comorbid mood and anxiety disorders don't sound like the recipe for success to me. Would you agree?

Emotional expression plays a big role in our relationships with others because it impacts how we communicate and behave. The better we know ourselves and our emotions, the better we can communicate our needs, avoid or correct misunderstandings, and improve the relationships that can impact our performance at work.

Let me ask you this, "Are you one of those people who thinks you should keep work and home separate so the two don't influence each other?" If so, I encourage you to look at the data I presented in Chapter Three and here. Consider how improving your emotional expression can improve your professional relationships. The benefits are universal, but if it helps to focus on workplace wins first, go for it!

If you and the people in your personal life are struggling to get on the same page or can't seem to address the issues on your own, would you consider a relationship counselor? If this other party is not your romantic partner, consider a mediator to help you improve your relationship with more effective communication.

Does how you express or suppress emotions cause challenges for you in your personal relationships? If you answered yes, you're in good company. Unfortunately, many of these challenges are rooted in misunderstandings, and it snowballs from there if we cannot find common ground. So, how can we take accountability and play a role in rectifying misunderstandings about how we express our emotions? Here's one way:

What is one thing you wish the people in your life knew about your emotional expression? Write it in the space below.

_____

_____

_____

_____

Try showing this to one or two of your most trusted loved ones. See if you can open a dialogue about how you want to optimize your emotional expression for the benefit of the relationship. You can repeat this exercise as often as you like (every week, two weeks, month, etc.) to help maintain good communication and understanding within your relationships for the long term.

It can be hard to start conversations like this because it is uncomfortable for some people to talk about their feelings. Use this exercise as a gateway. If you don't want to rip this page out to show them, could you write a text message or even an old-fashioned letter? What type of communication is less intimidating for you? A point to consider: if you fear this person won't understand you on the deeper level you require, despite your best efforts to communicate your emotions, are you sure they're the right person for your tribe?

📋 IN SUMMARY

In this chapter, you have learned how emotional expression can differ between those with ADHD and those without, how to put your passion to work, how to chase catharsis, why we need support and why a better me means a better we. I want you to stop thinking of your emotions as the enemy. Do not repress, suppress or avoid them. Do the work to learn about your emotions and explore ways to express them. Healthy emotional outlets and productive emotional expression will serve your progress as a leader. Now you know why mastering emotional expression as an ADHD leader is so important. We're almost done; hang in there. I am so proud of you for making it this far!

Conclusion

What a journey we've taken! I hope you feel energized, inspired, and primed to accomplish everything you want. You have learned how to recognize if you have ADHD and how to make it work optimally for you as a leader. We discussed everything from what your experience looked and felt like with undiagnosed or late diagnosis ADHD, how to seek diagnosis, and how to use the knowledge of your bullet-train brain to move you forward.

You now have tools built for you and a fresh perspective to reflect on your leadership journey. You are ready to move upward to even bigger successes. Imagine all of your hardships turning to home runs. Imagine leveraging what you were told were your weaknesses to turn them into your biggest strengths as a leader. Imagine your out-of-the-box thinking and unique perspective being celebrated instead of chastised. You don't have to just imagine it anymore. All of this and more is possible when you harness your ADHD and make it work for you. As they say, if you've got it, flaunt it!

You cannot optimize your brain function and the resulting communication and behaviors if you do not first understand how your brain works. So, here are your next steps:

1. Read and reread the first three chapters as often as you need to in order to understand your neurodiverse mind.
2. Seek a diagnosis if you do not already have one.
3. Use what you now know to reflect on where you've come from and where you want to go.
4. Implement the tools I provided in this book to start growing today.
5. Cultivate healthy habits for your body to fuel your mind.
6. Lean into your strengths and seek support for your weaknesses.
7. Use your emotions to achieve a depth of rapport and professional relationship that non-ADHDers might not be capable of.
8. Seek out a community of other neurodiverse professionals to add to your tribe.

If you have lived this long with undiagnosed or late diagnosis ADHD, there has probably been a lot of shame in your life and your leadership journey. You may have a hard time shaking off the weight of expectations from the neurotypical world, but now is your time to fly. You know what makes you tick, so use your unique capabilities to go out there and show them why you're the bomb (I can't help myself with the corny puns, but if you made it this far, maybe you enjoy lame jokes too!).

Conclusion

Nothing is more important in life than to help lift others up and make their journeys easier. I would love to hear about your experiences, how this book impacted or influenced you, and your plans for the future. Join me in a worldwide network of ADHD professionals and leaders at the END Institute (contact information in the next section). There you will find access to resources, community, and support as well as training and education. As you move into this next amazing chapter of your life with the clarity, knowledge and tools you have gained here, never forget the amazing things you are capable of.

After so much hardship, I wish you an unburdened soul, a mind at peace, and a leadership journey paved with all the successes you never thought possible until now. I hope you will never again feel as though you are unfit because you, shining little star that you are, were never made to fit in; you were made to stand out.

Invitation to Connect

I would love to hear from you! If you want to talk about the book, share your experiences, or inquire about speaking events, training, online programs, all the relevant contact information for myself and the END Institute is listed below.

Find me at:
- Email: info@endinstitute.com
- Call/text: 210-617-3461
- LinkedIn: "Gwendolyn Janssen MHA, MSN, RN"

Find the END Institute at:
- Website: https://endinstitute.com
- Email: info@endinstitute.com
- Call/text: 833-919-0957
- Facebook Private Group: "END Institute"
- LinkedIn Private Group: "Excellence in Neurodiversity (END) Institute"
- Instagram: @endinstitute

Connect with other experts

If you are interested in reaching out to any of the experts who generously provided insight and knowledge for some of this content, their contact information is below (in alphabetical order by last name).

Andrew Bordt M.Ed. Licensed educator and co-founder of The Institute for the Advancement of Group Therapy:
- 800-396-9927
- certification@grouptherapycertification.com
- https://grouptherapycertification.com

George Eastwood. Certified personal trainer and founder of The Neurodivergent PT:
- +447387184356
- thendcoach@outlook.com
- thendcoach.com
- Instagram: @theneurodivergentpt

Becca King MS, RDN, LDN. Dietitian, nutritionist and founder of ADHD Nutritionist LLC:
- 980-272-8250
- adhdnutritionist@gmail.com
- adhdnutritionistllc.com
- Instagram: @adhd.nutritionist

Brooke Schnittman MA, BCC, PCC. ADHD coach, public speaker, and founder of Coaching with Brooke:

- 561-303-2791
- brooke@coachingwithbrooke.com
- coachingwithbrooke.com
- Instagram: @coachingwithbrooke

Additional Resources

Attention Deficit Disorder Association (ADDA): add.org

Children and Adults with Attention-Deficit/Hyperactivity Disorder (CHADD): chadd.org

ADDitute magazine: additudemag.com

American Psychiatric Association: psychiatry.org

Psychology Today: psychologytoday.com/us

Bibliography

ADDA Editorial Team. "The Body Double: A Unique Tool for Getting Things Done." ADDA – Attention Deficit Disorder Association, October 24, 2022. https://add.org/the-body-double

ADDitude Editors. "ADHD Statistics: New ADD Facts and Research." *ADDitude*. July 13, 2022. www.additudemag.com/statistics-of-adhd

ADDitude Editors. "Change Your Diet, Find Your Focus." *ADDitude*. April 1, 2022. www.additudemag.com/can-the-right-diet-ease-add-symptoms

ADDitude Editors, and Ph.D. Carl Sherman. "What Causes ADHD? Culture vs. Biology." *ADDitude*. December 27, 2022. www.additudemag.com/what-causes-adhd-symptoms

ADHDadultUK. "FAQ about ADHD." September 25, 2022. www.adhdadult.uk/faq

American Psychiatric Association. *Diagnostic and Statistical Manual of Mental Disorders: DSM-5.* (Arlington, TX: American Psychiatric Association Publishing, 2013).

Bailey, Eileen. "Improve Working Memory: Brain Training Tricks." *ADDitude*, July 13, 2022. www.additudemag.com/improve-working-memory

Barkley, Russell A., and Mariellen Fischer. "Hyperactive Child Syndrome and Estimated Life Expectancy at Young Adult Follow-up: The Role of

ADHD Persistence and Other Potential Predictors." *Journal of Attention Disorders* 23, no. 9 (December 10, 2018): 907–23. https://doi.org/10.1177/1087054718816164

Barkley, Russell. "What Is Executive Function? 7 Deficits Tied to ADHD." *ADDitude*, October 29, 2022. www.additudemag.com/7-executive-function-deficits-linked-to-adhd

Ben-Dor Cohen, Maayan, Eran Eldar, Adina Maeir, and Mor Nahum. "Emotional Dysregulation and Health Related Quality of Life in Young Adults with ADHD: A Cross Sectional Study." *Health and Quality of Life Outcomes* 19, no. 1 (2021). https://doi.org/10.1186/s12955-021-01904-8

Centers for Disease Control and Prevention (CDC). "How much physical activity do adults need?". *U.S. Department of Health & Human Services.* June 2, 2022. www.cdc.gov/physicalactivity/basics/adults/index.htm

CHADD (Children and Adults with Attention-Deficit/Hyperactivity Disorder). "About ADHD – Overview." June 13, 2019. https://chadd.org/about-adhd/overview

CHADD (Children and Adults with Attention-Deficit/Hyperactivity Disorder). "Could a Body Double Help You Increase Your Productivity?" April 21, 2022. https://chadd.org/adhd-news/adhd-news-adults/could-a-body-double-help-you-increase-your-productivity

CHADD (Children and Adults with Attention-Deficit/Hyperactivity Disorder). "More Fire than Water: A Short History of ADHD." *ADHD Weekly.* October 23, 2018. https://chadd.org/adhd-weekly/more-fire-than-water-a-short-history-of-adhd

CHADD (Children and Adults with Attention-Deficit/Hyperactivity Disorder). "Relationships & Social Skills." December 21, 2018. https://chadd.org/for-adults/relationships-social-skills

Christian, Alex. "The Case for Job Hopping." *BBC Worklife.* BBC, July 21, 2022. www.bbc.com/worklife/article/20220720-the-case-for-job-hopping

Chung, Winston, Sheng-Fang Jiang, Diana Paksarian, Aki Nikolaidis, F. Xavier Castellanos, Kathleen R. Merikangas, and Michael P. Milham. "Trends in the Prevalence and Incidence of Attention-Deficit/Hyperactivity Disorder among Adults and Children of Different Racial and Ethnic Groups." *JAMA Network Open* 2, no. 11 (November 1, 2019). https://doi.org/10.1001/jamanetworkopen.2019.14344

Cleveland Clinic. "Rejection Sensitive Dysphoria (RSD)." August 30, 2022. https://my.clevelandclinic.org/health/diseases/24099-rejection-sensitive-dysphoria-rsd

Dodson, William M.D. "How Adults with ADHD Think: Uncomfortable Truths about the ADHD Nervous System." *ADDitude*, July 11, 2022. www.additudemag.com/adhd-in-adults-nervous-system

Flippin, Royce. "Hyperfocus: The ADHD Phenomenon of Intense Fixation." *ADDitude*, July 11, 2023. www.additudemag.com/understanding-adhd-hyperfocus

Gilman, Lois. "How to Succeed in Business with ADHD." *ADDitude*, February 18, 2021. www.additudemag.com/adhd-entrepreneur-stories-jetblue-kinkos-jupitermedia

Ginsberg, Ylva, Javier Quintero, Ernie Anand, Marta Casillas, and Himanshu P. Upadhyaya. "Underdiagnosis of Attention-Deficit/Hyperactivity Disorder in Adult Patients." *The Primary Care Companion For CNS Disorders*, June 12, 2014. https://doi.org/10.4088/pcc.13r01600

Grawert, Lauren. "Regular Exercise Benefits Both Mind and Body: A Psychiatrist Explains." Permanente Medicine, December 22, 2021. https://mydoctor.kaiserpermanente.org/mas/news/regular-exercise-benefits-both-mind-and-body-a-psychiatrist-explains-1903986

Gronewold, Janine, and Miriam Engels. "The Lonely Brain – Associations between Social Isolation and (Cerebro-) Vascular Disease from the Perspective of Social Neuroscience." *Frontiers in Integrative Neuroscience* 16 (January 28, 2022). https://doi.org/10.3389/fnint.2022.729621

Jakobi, Babette, Alejandro Arias-Vasquez, Erno Hermans, Priscilla Vlaming, Jan Buitelaar, Barbara Franke, Martine Hoogman, and Daan van Rooij. "Neural Correlates of Reactive Aggression in Adult Attention-Deficit/Hyperactivity Disorder." *Frontiers in Psychiatry* 13 (May 19, 2022). https://doi.org/10.3389/fpsyt.2022.840095

Johns Hopkins Medicine. "Attention-Deficit / Hyperactivity Disorder (ADHD) in Children." The Johns Hopkins University. n.d. www.hopkinsmedicine. org/health/conditions-and-diseases/adhdadd

Li, Ray. "Stop trying to convince people who don't believe in you . . ." LinkedIn. 2022. www.linkedin.com/posts/rayxli_stop-trying-to-convince-people-who-dont-activity-6977305235845246976-ASXm/?originalSubdomain=id

Lunsford-Avery, Jessica R., and Scott H. Kollins. "Delayed Circadian Rhythm Phase: A Cause of Late-Onset Attention-Deficit/Hyperactivity Disorder among Adolescents?" *Journal of Child Psychology and Psychiatry* 59, no. 12 (December, 2018): 1248–51. https://doi.org/10.1111/jcpp.12956

Marshburn, Christopher K., Kevin J. Cochran, Elinor Flynn, and Linda J. Levine. "Workplace Anger Costs Women Irrespective of Race." *Frontiers in Psychology* 11 (November 6, 2020). https://doi.org/10.3389/fpsyg.2020.579884

Mayo Clinic Staff. "Attention-deficit/hyperactivity disorder (ADHD) in children." *Mayo Clinic*. Mayo Foundation for Medical Education and Research (MFMER). June 25, 2019. www.mayoclinic.org/diseases-conditions/adhd/symptoms-causes/syc-20350889

Mayo Clinic Staff. "Cognitive behavioral therapy." *Mayo Clinic*. Mayo Foundation for Medical Education and Research (MFMER). March 16, 2019. www.mayoclinic.org/tests-procedures/cognitive-behavioral-therapy/about/pac-20384610

Nylander, Elin, Orestis Floros, Timea Sparding, Eleonore Rydén, Stefan Hansen, and Mikael Landén. "Five-Year Outcomes of ADHD Diagnosed in Adulthood." *Scandinavian Journal of Psychology* 62, no. 1 (2021): 13–24. https://doi.org/10.1111/sjop.12692

Orrie, Dan, Ami Cohen, Kfir Asraf, Ivgeny Saveliev, and Iris Haimov. "The Impact of Sleep Deprivation on Continuous Performance Task among Young Men with ADHD." *Journal of Attention Disorders* 25, no. 9 (January 9, 2020): 1284–94. https://doi.org/10.1177/1087054719897811

Park, Sabrina. "11 Bad*Ss Women Who Are Thriving with ADHD." *POPSUGAR Fitness*, May 25, 2019. www.popsugar.com/fitness/Famous-Women-ADHD-46084806

Ratey, John. "The ADHD Exercise Solution." *ADDitude*, March 17, 2020. www.additudemag.com/the-adhd-exercise-solution

Substance Abuse and Mental Health Services Administration (SAMHSA). "Adults with Attention Deficit Hyperactivity Disorder and Substance Use Disorders." U.S. Department of Health and Human Services vol. 14, no. 3 (November 2015). https://store.samhsa.gov/sites/default/files/d7/priv/sma15-4925.pdf

Seay, Bob, Bob Seay, Nancy Ratey, and Verified. "The ADHD-Dopamine Link: Why You Crave Sugar and Carbs." *ADDitude*, April 10, 2022. www.additudemag.com/slideshows/adhd-obesity-link

Shapiro, Scott S. "Adult ADHD and Work: Improving Executive Function." *Psychology Today*. (Sussex Publishers, January 20, 2016). www.psychology today.com/us/blog/the-best-strategies-managing-adult-adhd/201601/adult-adhd-and-work-improving-executive-function

Shapiro, Scott S. "Executive Function and ADHD." Scott Shapiro, MD – Adult ADD + ADHD NYC Psychiatrist, December 5, 2019. www.scottshapiromd.com/how-to-thrive-at-work-with-adhd

Sherman, Carl. "IS ADHD a Disability? Your Legal Rights at Work." *ADDitude*, May 26, 2022. www.additudemag.com/workplace-legal-protection

Sibley, Margaret H., L. Eugene Arnold, James M. Swanson, Lily T. Hechtman, Traci M. Kennedy, Elizabeth Owens, Brooke S.G. Molina, et al. "Variable Patterns of Remission from ADHD in the Multimodal Treatment Study of ADHD." *American Journal of Psychiatry* 179, no. 2 (February 2022): 142–51. https://doi.org/10.1176/appi.ajp.2021.21010032

Silver, Larry, M.D. "ADHD Medication Options: Stimulants, Nonstimulants & More." *ADDitude*, November 17, 2022. www.additudemag.com/adhd-medication-for-adults-and-children

The Global Handwashing Partnership. "About handwashing. History." 2017. https://globalhandwashing.org/about-handwashing/history-of-handwashing

Thorell, Lisa B., Hanna Tilling, and Douglas Sjöwall. "Emotion Dysregulation in Adult ADHD: Introducing the Comprehensive Emotion Regulation Inventory (CERI)." *Journal of Clinical and Experimental Neuropsychology* 42, no. 7 (July 18, 2020): 747–58. https://doi.org/10.1080/13803395.2020.1800595

Turner, Lea. "I'd never received any training before I hosted my first training session . . ." LinkedIn. 2022. www.linkedin.com/posts/lea-turner_id-never-received-any-training-before-i-activity-6998932542259085312-v8E1/ ?utm_source=share&utm_medium=member_desktop

Vos, Melissa, and Catharina A Hartman. "The Decreasing Prevalence of ADHD across the Adult Lifespan Confirmed." *Journal of Global Health* 12 (2022). https://doi.org/10.7189/jogh.12.03024

Wilding, Melody LMSW. 2022. "How to Use ADHD to Your Advantage, According to a Psychologist." Forbes. Forbes Magazine. www.forbes.com/ sites/melodywilding/2018/04/19/how-to-use-adhd-to-your-advantage/ ?sh=5bea388b7b5d

Wymbs, Brian T., Will H. Canu, Gina M. Sacchetti, and Loren M. Ranson. "Adult ADHD and Romantic Relationships: What We Know and What We Can Do to Help." *Journal of Marital and Family Therapy* 47, no. 3 (November 22, 2021): 664–81. https://doi.org/10.1111/jmft.12475

Young, S., D. Moss, O. Sedgwick, M. Fridman, and P. Hodgkins. "A Meta-Analysis of the Prevalence of Attention Deficit Hyperactivity Disorder in Incarcerated Populations." *Psychological Medicine* 45, no. 2 (April 7, 2014): 247–58. https://doi.org/10.1017/s0033291714000762

Zheng, Mark. "Why we started Sene. The Story of Ray and Mark." September 26, 2021. https://senestudio.com/pages/our-story

About the author

Gwen Janssen is a trained nurse with ADHD and autism, and a neurodiversity advocate, trainer, and educator. She was raised in upstate New York but currently lives in Texas with her two rescue dogs. She has always had a passion for caring for others, leading to her various roles in nursing, including leadership and education. However, there was always a feeling of disconnect on a level she could not understand. At 33, she was finally diagnosed with ADHD, helping her understand so many of her personal and professional struggles throughout her life. She has dedicated herself to improving awareness and support for those with ADHD and all types of neurodiversity in the workplace and society as a whole. She founded the END (Excellence in Neurodiversity) Institute to serve as a collaborative for neurodiverse professionals to share stories, tools, and tips to unlock potential and achieve success at work. Gwen hopes to be one of many global voices speaking, educating, and training to improve support for neurodiverse professionals everywhere.